·

TOM PHILBIN'S DO-IT-YOURSELF BARGAIN BOOK

ALSO BY TOM PHILBIN

TOM PHILBIN'S
DO-IT-YOURSELF
◀▶
BARGAIN BOOK

**How to Save 50%—and More—Buying Products
and Materials by America's #1 Do-It-Yourself Expert
and Author of *The Encyclopedia of Hardware***

WARNER BOOKS

A Time Warner Company

Warner Books, Inc., 1271 Avenue of the Americas, New York, NY 10020

W A Time Warner Company

Printed in the United States of America
First printing: May 1992
10 9 8 7 6 5 4 3 2 1

"All information contained in this book regarding brand name products is accurate as of December 1, 1991. As prices vary in different locales, price information is intended to be approximate, not exact."

Book design by Giorgetta Bell McRee
Cover design by Julia Kushnirsky
Cover photography by Tom Philbin III/Imagine Photography

To Mike, Bob, Nick and all my buddies at the Washington Drive Deli in Centerport, N.Y., and to my faithful friends at Pete's Used Auto Parts in Huntington, N.Y., Charley, Glenn and Don. The first group keeps *me* going, the second my car.

ACKNOWLEDGMENTS

My thanks to Mary and Hugh at Centerport Hardware; Don, Manny and John at Laurel Hardware in Northport; John Trench at A & B Hardware in Huntington; Charley Hudson of Allied Building Products; Nick DeRosa; Walter Hartten; Mark Rutter, President of Projects Plus in New Canaan, Connecticut; Ed Lindstadt of Lindstadt Gutters in Northport; Paul Sandberg of Freelance Garage Doors in Northport; and my profound thanks to Stan Zuba for introducing me to Dave Shannon, a hardware genius who, you might say, opened up new vistas for me in the world of nuts and bolts.

CONTENTS

INTRODUCTION

For as long as I've been writing on how-to subjects, I must admit that I still get a little buffaloed and dazzled by ads that seem to promise me the moon, lag screwwise. As if Circe were calling out to me, I am drawn to her chrome-covered island and think about reaching for my wallet.

Happily, I rarely get sucked in. I know better.

But I ask myself: What about the average person, the do-it-yourselfer? How much more vulnerable are they to the allure, the blandishments of the bozos who write the ads and slicksters who can make garbage look like fine jewelry? How much more easily can they be fooled than I?

A lot more.

This book will, I hope, make them invulnerable—or let's put it this way: a hell of a lot less vulnerable than they were before they picked it up.

I look at this book as a detailed battle plan for getting

bargains and getting your money's worth—which is many times a bargain.

In preparing it I must say that I did not underestimate, and this is not meant to be insulting, the lack of savvy—and the feeling of being overwhelmed by it all—of the average person who shops for diy (do-it-yourself) products and materials. You will not find, let us hope, generalities in this book. I get as specific as I possibly can. I name brand names. I give details on buying all kinds of specific products, including the kinds of money you can save and how. I give ballpark prices when practical so you'll get a better sense of what a good—or bad—buy an item is.

Details, concrete details, are, in my view, the only way to go. Like:

If you want a good stainless steel sink, buy the Elkay brand.

If you want tools that will save you a bundle there are many in the Fuller line that you can get.

If you want to save more than a hundred dollars on a Kohler toilet, shop around, ask for discounts.

In my mind's eye, I am sitting down at a table with you, having a cup of coffee, and you are asking me: "Tom, a caster on my couch broke. Where should I go to get a new one?"

Answer: "To a hardware store. Casters are sold two to four to the package, but a hardware store dealer will break open the package to give you just one—at one's price."

The book is filled with stuff like that.

I remember reading that Fyodor Dostoyevsky once said that, if at the end of Man's existence, God asks Man (or Woman) what he has learned for all the years he has lived, all that Man has to do is hand God a copy of *Don Quixote*.

Let me show you what bronze chutzpah is and put it this way: if God asks what you have learned about saving money when buying do-it-yourself products and materials, all you have to do is hand God a copy of *Tom Philbin's Do-It-Yourself Bargain Book.*

Don't laugh. You haven't read the book yet.

TOM PHILBIN

TOM PHILBIN'S
DO-IT-YOURSELF
BARGAIN BOOK

1

OVERALL SHOPPING TIPS

 Each of the chapters that follow will help you get some good—and in some cases wonderful—buys on things. The details are important to get the buys, but I think it's also a good idea to understand the buying principles that inform the chapters. If you can remember and apply some of these, you are bound to save some money—or a lot of money.

They are:

■ Carded items cost more than loose. More and more, companies are packaging items in so-called "carded" form, a piece of cardboard with the product retained by some sort of clear plastic blister.

In general, such items are 25 percent more than what

you'd pay loose. Carding has found its way into all diy (do-it-yourself) areas.

So, the idea is to buy loose whenever you can. And this includes boxed items. For some reason—and there may be exceptions—you don't pay for the box when you buy something, but you do pay for that infamous card.

■ Just about everything you can name comes loose. While the trend is toward carded, there are still outlets— particularly hardware stores—where you can get things loose. All you have to do is search.

■ Discounts are available on almost all products and materials. Maybe this should be written in neon, because it is a vitally important shopping tip—and it's a well-kept secret. The fact is that the manufacturer's suggested list, or the list price, is meaningless. You shouldn't expect to pay it—and you shouldn't.

The fact is that discounts are available on all kinds of products and materials from all kinds of outlets, including home centers and plumbing supply and electrical supply stores (once the exclusive province, discountwise, of the pros).

To get the discount, all you have to do is ask for it. Not: "Can you give me a discount?" but "What kind of discount do you offer?"

Every single retailer I talked with in researching this book said they gave discounts. The reason is simple: It's good business. They get the sale because they give the price, rather than staunchly standing behind a high price, and losing the sale.

Just how much off list you can get cannot be said with surety. It would depend, to some degree, how much the item's markup typically is, and how much the dealer has already marked it down. But just to give you a ballpark, overall sense of discounts, I would say that, starting with the list price, you could get 30 percent off windows (including Andersen and other good brands), 25 percent off bath fixtures, 50 percent off lighting fixtures, 10 percent off lumber and the basics, 10 percent to 15 percent off tools, and 30 percent to 40 percent off kitchen and bath cabinets.

The reason is simple: Many items have the markup to absorb a healthy discount and still yield a good profit for the retailer.

For example, general building supplies have a markup of 30 percent over a retailer's cost, general hardware 70 to 80 percent, bath fixtures 50 percent. Recently, for example, I was offered a 25 percent discount on a Kohler whirlpool, a savings of $150 and the dealer would still make that much himself.

Now you can't expect a discount on a $5 or $10 item, and I can't detail at just what point you can ask. But my sense is this: When an item gets above $30 it's time to start asking. And as the figure fattens so will the size of the discount.

■ Shop around. This is a tried and true method—and highly recommended. I can assure you that prices vary from outlet to outlet, and sometimes hugely. It can save you a lot on small items as well as large. And after a while you may find yourself frequenting one place, because that's where the best prices are.

Shopping around doesn't mean just store visits, though these are heartily recommended. Get used to looking at ads, picking up fliers, writing manufacturers for literature. And once you know exactly what you want, start shopping around using the phone as suggested in the box (page 5).

On some things—tools, particularly—you can also check some catalogs. We've got some winners with great prices, and you can use them as sort of a benchmark for your shopping. (See Box on page 151.)

■ You must know what you're buying. This is my job in the book, and I hope I do it, because you can't get a buy on an item unless you are in a position to know what you are purchasing when comparing prices. You have to compare apples to apples but you have to be sure that they're all apples.

Make sure of this, because it can get tricky. Kohler, for example, offers four toilets, all very different with various prices, and all named "Rialto."

■ Buying in bulk is not always best. Most of the time things sold in bulk will save you money. For example, the more screws and nails you buy, the more you'll save per pound.

But the key point is this: Unless you use it all you can lose.

I use myself as a prime example. Years ago, before I learned, I went into a plumbing supply store to get a washer for a leaky faucet. So when I asked the proprietor for a washer, he asked:

"Box of 100?"

"Sure," I said.

My question now is this: Anyone interested in buying a small box containing 97 flat red washers?

■ Some outlets will break open packages to sell a limited number of items. Most hardware stores will break open a package of a popular item if you just need one or two of a thing, and this can save you money. Casters and fuses are two such things that come to mind. This can save having the rest of the items go to waste, as it were.

■ The best quality is not always required—or desired. This concept is particularly evident when it comes to tools. However active do-it-yourselfers are, they don't always—even usually—need high-end tools because there are a number of lower-priced brands that will serve quite well.

■ Great buys are available at garage sales. It's true. Chapter 8 has the details.

■ Just about every part of every thing that exists can be replaced. Before you throw anything out, get the parts and repair it. That alone can save you a bundle.

SHOPPING AROUND:
SOME IMPORTANT POINTS

Shopping around is, of course, crucial to achieving great savings on diy products, but several points should be emphasized.

One: You can use the phone successfully.

Two: Use the Yellow Pages.

First, don't believe the myth that retailers won't give you a price over the phone. The vast majority will.

One way to do this is simply to call, ask if they have the item and then ask the price. It is important to know exactly what you want so you can transmit it to the clerk in language he or she understands; in some cases (such as bath fixtures, light fixtures, power tools) knowing the model number will be essential.

In almost all cases I predict that you will get the price, particularly granted recessionary times.

If you are chary about being so direct, then you can be a little more artful in your query. Following is something I use (some days I don't feel too direct).

First, ask if the retailer has such and such product, even if you know that it's highly likely they do. Play dumb.

When they say yes, then you say:

"How much would that cost?"

Invariably, you'll get the answer, which sometimes

will involve the retailer going back to the product to get the price.

Don't ask me why they give the information. Maybe it's because the focus of the first question is not on price but product, and maybe it's because I don't make it sound like I know precisely about such things. Whatever, it's a technique I've used successfully for many years.

Sometimes, when they won't give the price I go into technique No. 2 which is: "I would really appreciate knowing the cost. I don't want to travel over there if I can't afford it."

This tactic pulled the info out of a number of retailers.

I also strongly suggest you use the Yellow Pages—and call and call—and call some more—until you feel you have the best price. As detailed in the book, retail price doesn't exist and the savings can be phenomenal.

Incidentally, there's no reason why you can't call wholesale outlets for products and prices. All they can do is say no—and sometimes they say yes, and you can make out quite well.

2

SAVING ON GENERAL HARDWARE

 As public relations specialists Deb Hagen pointed out to me during the writing of this book, I should tell you not to forget that "pennies" add up.

Indeed, I can testify to the validity of that. Even small savings on individual items can become significant, particularly if they're used over and over again.

Perhaps nowhere is this more evident than in the area of general hardware... the nuts, bolts, screws, nails, etc., that constitute what might be called hardcore hardware. Some of these items are used repeatedly by active do-it-yourselfers, and even over a year pennies can turn to dollars, even hundreds of dollars saved.

Generally speaking, you'll do better at home centers when shopping for general hardware than at hardware stores or building supply or lumber yards. The latter two tend to have even higher prices than hardware stores. On the other hand, I am not a purist. I will not travel three miles to save a dollar. I head for the hardware store. But in my area I have the luxury of going to any of four, two really close by, so I can pick the cheapest of these.

No matter what outlet you go to, as I mentioned in the overall tips section, one key to saving on hardware is to buy loose whenever you can, rather than carded. Carded is always more expensive. For example, during a recent foray to a hardware store I saw a package of braces on sale for $1.69; the same bought loose—and these were in the same store—cost $1.15, including screws.

One big advantage hardware stores have over other outlets, aside from, in most cases, convenience, is that if you need just one of an item, as mentioned earlier, a dealer might well break open a package to give it to you—and sell the rest singly to other customers.

Finally, some hardware stores carry old items—with old prices. More than once I have come across an item with a faded label and an equally faded price.

Braces

Braces—that is, T plates, mending plates, corner irons, etc.—are used to strengthen loose joints on such things as garage doors and screen doors. The brace is placed so it overlaps the loose parts and then is screwed in place so the parts can't move.

Braces come in two basic qualities: Stanley and everyone else. Stanley makes high-quality braces with finely finished countersunk screwholes that are made of extra-

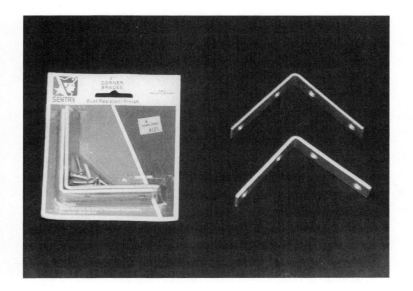

Packaged braces here cost $1.69. Loose braces cost a buck plus screws—maybe 15 cents. Time after time, loose beats carded prices.

strong metal. If you have a special job then these would be the way to go.

For most jobs, however, it's much more economical to buy other brands. Stanley's braces are carded; buy the carded Ferum brand and you can save 10 percent to 15 percent. Such braces will do the job; I use them all the time. They come with and without screws.

To save even more money, buy loose. These are braces that dealers keep on hooks and in a wide variety of sizes. Here, you can save up to 25 percent over Stanley's carded types, and a nice hunk over other carded brands. If you buy loose, you must purchase screws separately, which won't significantly erode the savings to be made.

If you have a need for a lot of the same kind of braces

you can also buy them in bulk in boxes. The number of braces in the box will depend on the particular size (braces come in a wide variety of sizes) and types; the bigger they are, the fewer per box. If buying a box, you can usually get a discount of up to 20 percent over loose (at this rate the dealer will be paying you to remove them from his store).

Cabinet Hardware

Cabinet hardware—that is, hinges, catches, knobs and pulls—comes carded, loose and in bulk. Buy loose when you can, but if you need a fair number of these items, buy a box full. Most companies sell hinges 10 to a box and you can save around 15 percent if you buy this way. Catches come 20 to the box and you can save a similar amount. Knobs come 25 to the box, each individually wrapped, and buying this way will chalk up around 10 percent in savings.

If you are doing a fairly big job and need, say, eight hinges rather than a full box (10), consider buying the entire box anyway. You might need a hinge or two down the road, and this way you'll have the exact style needed— and at today's prices.

You can save on hinges, also, by sticking to chrome ones rather than those that are brass-plated or, even more costly, pure brass.

Cable

Here I'm talking about multiple strand wire that looks like rope only it's made of wire and is a thousand times stronger. It is available in a variety of sizes and strengths and some is covered with a transparent plastic sheathing.

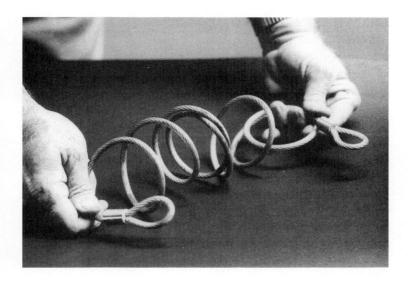

Cable. Cheapest way to buy this is by the foot off a roll.

Some cable comes packaged, but it is usually sold by the foot off rolls. You can also get it prepared in certain lengths for specific uses, such as for dog runs and for garage doors.

The cheapest way to buy it is by the foot off a roll, buying just what you need. If necessary, it can be bought in 250-foot rolls, interconnected in 50′ lengths which can be readily broken at the 50′ marks. This way you can save at least 10 percent.

Casters

Caster wheels occasionally crack and need to be replaced. The way to save here is to buy a single replacement caster (or two) rather than an entire package which contains two to four casters.

Savings can be good. For example, a few months ago I bought one 2½″ plate type furniture caster rather than the two in the package. The pair was priced at $10.69 and I only paid half that, a saving of over $5.00.

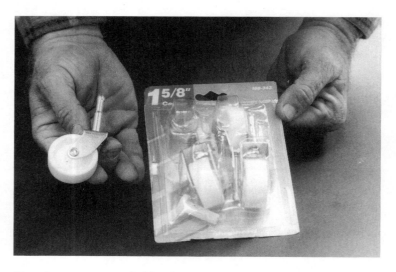

Need one caster? Hardware store dealers will usually break open a package to sell you just one so you won't have extras rolling around your house.

Hardware stores generally carry a nice array of casters and will likely have what you need. A home center will probably be unwilling to break open a package of casters for you, however, because their computers would not know how to react to such an aberration as someone selling just part of the package's contents.

Chain

Chain can be purchased packaged for specific uses such as dog runs or swing sets, but the cheapest way to buy it, like cable, is by the foot off a roll.

Chain comes in many different strengths (called SWL or Safe Working Load), and the stronger it is the more you pay. Hence it's a good idea to carefully match the job to chain strength. A friend of mine once told me of buying some chain to pull some tree stumps along the ground. "Later I discovered," he said, "that the guy had sold me Grade 30 proof coil chain with an SWL of thousands of pounds, which was strong enough to pull a freight train across my yard!"

Also, chain comes plain and galvanized; galvanized costs lots more. If you don't need weatherproof chain, don't get it. On the other hand, if you are using chain in an outside application and want it to last, then galvanized is suggested: it will last for decades while its non-galvanized relation will readily rust out.

Chain Accessories

There are a number of useful accessories to use with chain, but for saving money the most useful types are mash links and cold shuts, which are connectors and allow you to link lengths of chain. Connecting links are also very useful. Hence, if you have some old short lengths of chain around but need a longer length for a particular use, these connectors can serve well. Just make sure the one or ones you use are as strong as the links. Like they say, a chain is only as strong as its weakest link.

Connecting link like this can make a useless chain useful.

Mash links and cold shuts and the like cost a few dollars or so, depending on the size you buy, but it's a small price to make an unusable chain usable.

Closet Door Hardware

When sliding door hardware goes bad it's usually the rollers, guides or wheels rather than the track, and all these things are individually replaceable.

Sizes are standard and Stanley makes replacement

parts that will be properly sized most of the time. If Stanley doesn't fit (always bring the part to the store to show the dealer), then the dealer can look for something else for you that will fit.

Door Locks

For interior doors, I prefer using locks that can fit a standard 2⅛″ hole. Any number of standard locks can be fit into a hole this size sometime in the future, should it become necessary.

I would suggest you get the Kwikset brass-plated all-metal lock, in the 300 to 400 series. (Their Tylo model has some plastic parts.)

Kwikset all-metal entry lock, a good buy. Avoid the company's Tylo model, which has plastic parts.

Normally, your best bet for buying a lock would be home centers. They run sales three or four times a year, and the savings can be significant. For example I saw a Kwikset like the all-metal one shown here in a home center for $14.95—and I've seen the same lock for $25.00.

Some locks are very expensive, costing hundreds of dollars, and look like they were created in a factory that makes jewelry rather than hardware. But high price doesn't mean a better-quality lock. What you pay extra for—such as bath fixtures—is style.

Keys for locks also vary significantly in price, and the markup is vast. My friend Dave Shannon, who worked in a hardware store for years, says the blanks cost around 13¢; even top-of-the line nickel-plated ones only cost 17¢... and we all know that you pay at least $1 for a new key.

My experience getting keys made is dismal. Half the time they don't work. I did have good luck at Sears, but the price was $2.29 per, which is highway robbery. On the other hand, it saved me time, gas and aggravation.

Drawer Hardware

Here, I mean drawer track, the track that the drawer slides on either on the sides or down the center.

Most stores sell best-selling versions of drawer track, and you may be able to get bargains by comparison shopping. But an even easier way to a good buy might be to check out the Woodworkers' Supply catalog (see Chapter 9). In it I've seen track at good prices, though not sensational, but you will save time and effort not having to traipse around looking for the hardware.

There are also drawings in the catalog which will help

you determine if the track for sale will fit your particular drawer.

Framing Fasteners

These devices, which are formed sections of galvanized sheet metal, are for joining framing members. They are available individually or in cartons of 25 and 50 pieces. Buying by the carton is much cheaper: you'll save about 50 percent... and these hangers are not cheap. For example, a pair of joist hangers was priced for 45 cents.

The best-known brand is Teco—in fact, on jobs framing fasteners are called Tecos—but other brands are available at lower cost. Check them out for price (and quality).

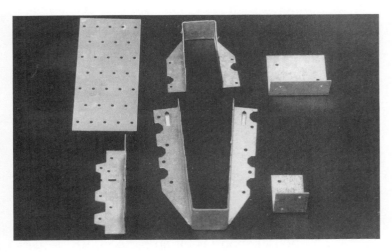

Framing fasteners. These are expensive but you can save 50 percent by buying them by the box, assuming you need a lot.

Note that framing fasteners may represent overkill in terms of strength required. They make a structure super strong, but under normal stresses they may not be needed: unless you are in an area where violent weather is the norm, you may decide that their strength is not required.

Garage Door Hardware

Just about all garage door hardware components are replaceable. Following is an array with details on replacing them, and, in a couple of instances, how to make your own hardware and save even more.

■ Cable. A garage door has two cables, but normally only one breaks. Manufacturers, though, sell replacement cable kits which contain *two* cables plus clips. You can buy this (or ask the dealer to sell you one) but who knows when, if ever, you will use the second cable. And a pair of cables might cost around $8.00.

A better bet is to buy your own cable loose. Just show the dealer the cable so he can give you the right size. Use the old cable as a guide for attaching the clip, which will form the necessary eye in the end of the cable for attachment.

Making your own can easily save you $3 to $4.

■ Spring. These come in four different capacities.

A 95-pound spring handles a fiberglass door; a 135-pound spring is for a single new wood overhead door; a 150-pound spring is for an old door (these were made heavier than new ones); and a 210-pound spring is for a 16' door.

To get a replacement, simply show the old spring to

the dealer. Or, you may be able to use the existing spring if you want to expend some extra effort. Usually, the end of the spring breaks off. To remedy this, first heat the end to cherry red with a propane torch for about 10 minutes, then bend the coil into the necessary hook shape. You'll save yourself anywhere from $10 to $25 depending on the size of the spring.

Garage door spring. When it breaks it usually does so at one end. The existing coil can be bent and save you the $10 to $25 a new one would cost.

Handles, wheels, rollers and guides are also available and come in standard sizes. Again, show the existing part to the dealer.

If the garage door is coming apart it, too, can be resuscitated. Sometimes doors start coming apart at the panels, and it is an easy matter to use heavy strap hinges (usually available loose) to tie the panels together from the inside. If the bottom is coming apart, it can be resecured with a pair of framing-fastener nailing plates, which are flat pieces of galvanized metal peppered with nail holes. (See page 17).

Hardware Cloth

This is a very tough screen-like material with a variety of uses around the home, for instance as a sand sifter or cage material.

Hardware cloth comes 2' to 4' wide and is sold by the foot, cut off a roll. It comes in various meshes, but the key consideration in buying it is that you get what you pay for. There are two kinds of galvanized hardware cloth: that which is galvanized after the cloth is made, and that which is woven of pre-galvanized wire. The pre-galvanized material is inferior because when the

Galvanized hardware cloth. Good stuff is shown here. Don't pay good prices for bad hardware cloth.

strands of wire are assembled to form the cloth by spot welding, the zinc is burned off the points where it welded, and the metal is subject at these points to attack from weather.

Hardware cloth with ½" squares and 36" wide would cost around $2.50 a foot.

Hinges

When buying interior door hinges, the best way to save is to buy and use standard interior hinges, such as 3" × 3", 3½" × 3½"—the sizes refer to the depth of the hinge. Sometime down the road you may need a replacement hinge. They will likely be easy to find and it's likely that cost will have held the line. Also, installing standard hinges is easier than installing oddball ones.

Hinges come carded, or as a pair loose in a box. A box is about 5 percent cheaper.

Exterior doors get a lot of abuse, much more than interior types, so they are normally hung with three hinges rather than just two. This means that to get three hinges you may have to buy four, and one—called half a pair in the trade—will go to waste. Solution: ask the dealer to sell you half a pair. It can save you around $1.65.

Nails

Nails are always cheaper when bought in bulk: the more you buy, the more you save.

The most popular size is in a one-pound box, but it's usually better to get them loose. If you need a lot of nails, you can also obtain them in 50-pound cartons.

Nuts and Bolts

This is one area where I've seen hardware outrageously overpriced. A few nuts and bolts are packed into a blister package and then sold for a dollar or two, whereas if you bought the bolt loose, it would cost maybe one quarter of the price. For example, in one store I saw an array of carded nuts and bolts selling for $1.39. Some of the items bought loose would have cost 15 cents or so.

Hardware store dealers commonly have drawers containing all kinds and sizes of nuts and bolts and you can buy one or 20. Someone will package your purchase in a little brown bag.

Wall of shame. The dealer priced all of these carded items at $1.39. Some of the items bought loose would cost ten or fifteen cents.

If you need a lot of a particular item, buy them in bulk in a box. If a dealer doesn't have boxes on hand he can order them, and you'll save perhaps 25 percent.

It is here that one can clearly observe the extra cost of galvanized products. I picked up a ¼" × 4" lag bolt in The Home Depot which was selling for 33 cents in bright metal and 44 cents for the same size in a galvanized finish. That extra dime can add up: every 10 bolts is more than a dollar extra, so it bears repeating that the consumer should carefully evaluate whether the project requires weatherproof fasteners.

For overall savings, the active do-it-yourselfer should buy a box of ¼" × 2" stove bolts. These fasteners are threaded all the way to the slotted head and come with nuts. In this quantity savings are substantial, and the stove bolt is an all-purpose fastener for all kinds of jobs from repair of metal and wood items to assembling strap iron.

Stove bolts, very handy and inexpensive fasteners for the active do-it-yourselfer.

Rope

Rope and cord (which is defined as anything less that ¼" in diameter) is sold by the foot off reels and in packages of 25, 50 and 100 feet.

If you need a relatively short, specific length of rope, say 20 feet, then by all means buy it by the foot. However if you need a fairly substantial amount, the best way to buy, if you can, is by the package: it will turn out to be less costly per foot. For example, if you bought a 100-foot package of ¼" hemp it might cost you $6.50. But if you bought the same kind of rope loose by the foot it would cost you 11¢ a foot or $11. That's a difference of $5.50 for 100 feet.

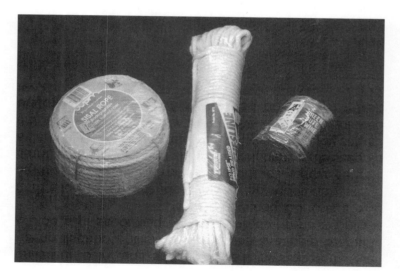

The cheapest way to buy rope and cord, unless you need a short, specific length, is by the package, as shown.

Many times rope is bought and not all of it is used immediately. The best way to save money in the long run is to ensure that the excess rope is stored *properly* so it will be in good shape when you need it. To do this, tie it in a hank and suspend it from the ceiling.

Rope Accessories

A variety of accessories are available for rope. Most are made of steel and are sold loose. But a good way to save is to buy plastic accessories when you can. One I like in particular is a thimble made of nylon. This works perfectly well, costs much less than steel, and also floats, a boon when using rope in water.

Screening

Three or four kinds of screening are available, and there are a number of ways to save.

Screening comes packaged and loose. Typically, packaged screening would be six feet long and in various widths up to 48″. Loose means cut off a 100-foot roll. It comes in various widths. You tell the dealer the length and width you need and he or she cuts it off the roll with shears.

Aluminum screening is most popular. When buying, be aware that it comes in two different gauges, heavy and light (18 × 16 and 18 × 14), and you don't want to be paying heavier gauge prices for lighter gauge material. Incidentally, the heavier (18 × 14) is excellent where kids are: it can take a hard hit much better than the lighter gauge material can.

These gauges come in bright aluminum, but there is

also a black anodized variety, which is the most transparent screening you can buy and the cheapest (it's cheap because so much of it is sold). It goes for around 45 cents to 50 cents a foot for 36" wide material.

The most expensive way to buy screening is in the package. This costs more per foot to begin with, and if you are left with material you can't use, you've wasted money.

BRONZE

■ If you live near the water, aluminum screening may be a poor investment. The salt can break it down fast. Better, though expensive, is bronze screening, which will not deteriorate under the assault of salt water.

A cheaper screening which can be used in the same situation is fiberglass, which comes in gray and black. Fiberglass looks fine and will last forever. Its only drawback is that it is not as strong. If something hits it, it can tear: the same object that hits heavy-gauge aluminum will bounce off it but will likely tear fiberglass. Hence, if you have kids cavorting (or playing like savages) in the area, think twice about fiberglass.

CHEAPER SPLINE

■ Spline is the flexible gasket that is pressed down into the grooves around metal-frame screens to hold the screening in place at the edges. Spline comes smooth and grooved and in various numbered sizes to fit various screens. You can buy it loose, in packages, and, if required, in 250-foot rolls. In many cases, when replacing screening, you can save the cost of new spline by using the old material: just wash it in warm soapy water. This cleans it but also makes it soft and flexible, easier to use.

SCREEN PATCHES

■ Sometimes screens get small holes in them which are an open invitation to bugs. For this you can buy small screen patches, but a cheaper alternative is to cut a small patch from extra screening you may have around.

On the other hand, getting a whole new piece of screening may be the way to go. I remember years ago when I saw another how-to guy on the Joan Rivers show demonstrating to her how to patch screening, and after a massive effort Joan gave him a bewildered look and asked:

"Why not just get a new screen?"

I remember guffawing. She may have had a point.

Screws

As with nuts and bolts, if you buy screws carded you will pay an inordinate amount of money for them. Manufacturers package 10 or 15 screws in a little blister pack and then charge you $1.29, which is giving you an extra screw free.

It's better to buy loose if you need only a few screws, and buy by the box if you need a lot.

Buying loose may mean that you only pay pennies for a screw. For example, I bought a dozen 1½" No. 6 Phillips head screws in a local hardware store and paid 35 cents. In a box, 100 of the same screws only cost $2.50, or 2.5 cents each. To put that another way, at that price rate you get 17 or 18 more screws for your money.

Here, again, take care before purchasing galvanized screws. They can cost a lot more.

Overall, I have found the bugle head (it's shaped like a bugle) drywall screw to be an excellent buy. It is very

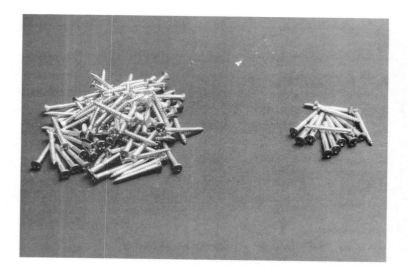

The more screws you buy, the less you pay. The dozen screws on the right cost 35 cents. The 100 on the left cost only $2.50, or an extra 18 screws.

cheap and can be used to secure a wide variety of wood members, as well as metal, and it requires no pilot holes. The drywall screw is easy to drive with a magnetic bit on a drill.

Screweyes and Screwhooks

These devices also come in packages and loose, and of course whenever you can, buy them loose (some dealers sell small ones packaged and big ones loose). Here, again, if you buy by the package you can end up getting more than you need and you'll have waste.

Shelf Supports

There are a number of supports for shelves.

One type is pilasters, small L-shaped devices which fit into slots in standards. The shelves, in turn, rest on the pilasters.

Pilasters are made of metal or plastic; plastic is cheaper. Plastic pilasters cost around 3 to 4 cents while metal costs 6 to 7 cents each. If you want to install glass shelves, you must get pilasters with holes for rubber plugs or grommets. The plugs are inserted in the pilaster so the glass can't shift. Such pilasters cost around 11 cents each plus 12 cents for the rubber plugs.

The utility bracket is another type of hanger designed to fit into a standard. They come in various qualities. Ferum is a common brand and so is Stanley; Stanley is of slightly higher quality and costs around 10 percent more. For most people, the Ferum brand will be fine.

Utility brackets are normally sold loose. Common sizes are 6″ × 8″ (the part the shelf rests on), 8″ × 10″ and 10″ × 12 ″.

Another bracket, which does the same thing as the utility bracket, is the shelf bracket, which is more finely made and comes cadmium plated, brass plated, antique-brass plated and black.

Such brackets also come loose and in varying qualities and costs. The standards in the industry, as it were, are the K-V and Keil brands. Cost is around $2.30 per bracket and $2.90 for a 3″-long standard.

Storm Door Hardware

Like garage doors, any part of a storm door's hardware can be replaced.

The main replacement piece is the pneumatic closer, of which there are perhaps six different kinds. Usually, when you first purchase the door, it is equipped with the manufacturer's top-of-the line closer, but if it goes bad there's no need for a top-of-the line replacement closer for, say, $12.98. Rather, you can get the standard Storm King or Ideal brand closer at a hardware store or other outlet for $8.98 and it will work well enough until you're ready to replace the door itself.

The same thing applies to chain and other storm door components. If you think it's worth it, you can also shop around a bit for better prices, though we are not talking megabucks savings here.

Wall Fasteners

For fastening things to walls and ceilings, a variety of devices are available.

Perhaps most closely associated with hanging things are hollow wall anchors, so called because they are designed to hang things on hollow wall material, i.e., drywall, commonly known by the brand name Sheetrock.

Molly is the most common name brand of wall fasteners, but others make them, too.

They come packaged and loose—and guess which is cheaper?

I priced a pair of large fasteners sold loose and they were 52 cents each. In a package, they were $1.79. The same thing would apply to toggle bolts and any other kind of fastener.

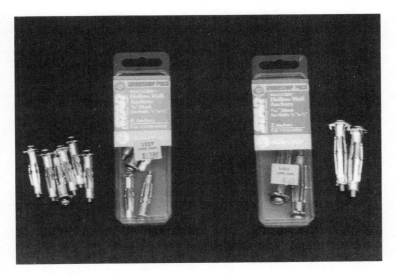

Hollow wall anchors, loose and carded. Six loose anchors at left cost a dollar; those in packages cost $1.79. Situation at right was even worse: two anchors loose cost $1, the packaged cost $1.79. In other words, if you bought carded, you would be paying 79 cents for the package.

There are also fasteners for concrete, including lead shields, and fiber and plastic shields. These are packed into a hole made in the concrete, and then a screw is run through the device to be hung and into the sleeve, which grips it tightly by the threads.

Here, the cheapest sleeves are the fiber and plastic kind. They work just as well as lead, and for a lot less.

One other product is of interest. This is lead wool, which looks like rough steelwood. It it actually lead which is packed into holes and then the screws are driven through the item into the hole. This is cost effective if you have a lot of things to hang on concrete. It is also very forgiving of holes that are not exactly in the right position. Screws driven in will nevertheless be held fast by the lead wool.

Window Hardware

There are many kinds of window hardware and it's the same story: prices will vary from outlet to outlet.

One particularly interesting piece, however, is window spring strips. These are wavy pieces of stainless steel and are designed to be inserted between window and track when the window's own hanging mechanism has failed.

These strips fill the gap between track and window and you can operate it normally. Thus, you can save an otherwise good window, or avoid replacing its hardware. The strips cost about $2 per pair.

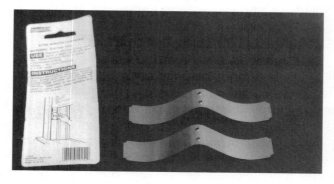

These spring devices, which cost all of $2, can save you having to buy new hardware to make a double-hung window work. Each strip is forced into the space between window and track to fill the gap and create friction that keeps the window operative.

3

SAVING ON HAND AND POWER TOOLS

 Large savings are possible on tools for the average do-it-yourselfer. In some cases, tools that are of decent but not top-notch quality can be bought at less than half the price of their more costly counterparts.

For example, you can get perfectly serviceable pipe wrenches from the Fuller Company at far less than half of what you'd pay for them from Ridgid. The main difference is that Ridgid is more suitable for a full-time plumber. Fuller guarantees their tools 100 percent under normal use. So if you break one, the manufacturer has instructed retailers to exchange it for a new one with no questions asked.

On the other hand, in some cases I would suggest only top-notch quality for the active do-it-yourselfer. You want to get good paintbrushes, rollers, chalk boxes and other items to avoid problems on the job where lesser quality can lead to extra work and problems. For example, cheap paintbrushes and rollers can have you picking hair and fiber out of wet paint.

At any rate, specific recommendations are made and the logic behind the recommendations is given in this chapter. You should quickly be able to decide whether you want to buy the specific tool suggested, or whether one of even lesser or better quality—and less or more money—will serve your needs best.

As in other chapters, average prices—my overall sense of what the tools usually cost—are given, but, of course, you can find them for less and for more.

Generally, hardware stores and lumberyards/building supply dealers charge the highest prices on tools, and home centers charge less. But, again, you may not want to trek over to a home center to save $2, say, and so will get the tool at the local hardware store.

One cheap outlet that we've found is in the Trendlines tool catalog, details of which are contained in Chapter 4. They carry brand name as well as good quality offbeat brand tools. Harbor Freight Tools also carries brand name tools as well as offbeat brands at very low cost.

With catalog shopping you may also save on sales tax if your state has it and if you shop interstate, and, possibly, shipping charges. If your order is over $50, from Harbor Freight the shipping is free. On the other hand, you have to pay for shipping if the order is below $50. For example, I recently saw a Stanley 25′ power tape on sale for $9.99 in the Harbor Freight catalog, which is a good price, but shipping would add $2.45 to the cost, which was still a lot less than two local hardware stores, one of which had the tool for almost $20, another for $16. (The Home Depot had it for $7.70.)

You can ask a hardware store or buildings supply

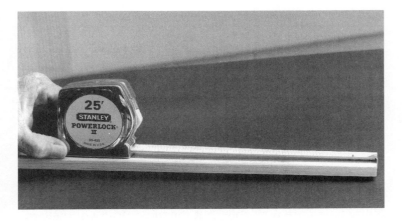

Shopping around pays. This tool was priced at around $20 in a local hardware store; $16 in another hardware store nearby—and *$7.70* in The Home Depot.

dealer for a 10 percent discount on any tool; it's likely that as the tool goes up in price the more likely he will be to grant it. Even with the discount, though, the price may be a lot higher than what you can get it for elsewhere.

Following is an array of tools some of which are essential, and some good to have, for the active do-it-yourselfer. If your local dealer doesn't have the tool, he can send for it.

HAND TOOLS

Caulking Guns

A few kinds are available, but for me the best is the half-barrel type with the ratchet plunger. As you squeeze the trigger, the plunger presses against the bottom of the caulking cartridge and forces it out. I like the gun because it's easy to get the cartridge in and out, and it's easy to stop the caulk flow; just flip the end of the plunger. It's a good idea to get a decent caulking gun; for a good quality one expect to pay around $3.75.

Cement Finishing Tools

Many types are available, but for most do-it-yourselfers I think only two types are needed: a small pointing trowel which can be used to apply mortar to block or brick, and a brick trowel for applying mortar when building. A good brand is Marshalltown. The brick trowel goes for $15 to $18 and the pointing trowel around $6. If you don't get a Marshalltown pointing trowel, make sure that the blade flexes; if it doesn't flex the quality is poor.

Center Punches

This tool is used for making depressions in metal for easier starting of a drilling operation. One good brand is General and it goes from $1.65 to $1.90. You want something with hard steel, which this has.

A close cousin of the center punch is the nailset, which is used with a hammer to countersink, or depress, nail heads beneath the surface of the wood. Mayhew makes a good one for around $2.30.

Chalk Boxes

Here, staying with high-line quality is best. Straight-line is a good one. The cord they use is strong, it holds chalk well and it's easy to get chalk refills. Cost: $3.70 for a 50-footer.

Chisels

For wood, only a chisel ⅜" × 4" long with a metal cap is recommended. Since it takes a lot of punishment—pounding with a hammer—better quality is recommended. Stanley makes a good one for around $10.

A cold chisel for working on metal and masonry is also a good idea. A 1"-wide tool is good. Enders makes a good one that will hold its edge quite nicely. And this is important. Some cold chisels look good but the edge gets dull after being used a couple of times. The Enders chisel costs around $9.50.

A good metal-capped wood chisel is suggested. Stanley makes a good one for about $10.

Coping Saws

Coping saws with square, rigid frames are better than ones with round frames that can bind and break. Stanley and Great Neck make good ones. Average cost is around $10.

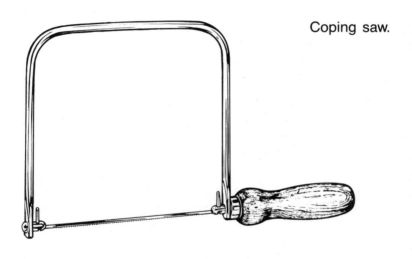

Coping saw.

Files/Rasps

Some people think files are used only for metal and rasps only for wood, but all you really need is one file of a specific size and style. I would suggest an 8″ half round (half a circle in profile) with a so-called bastard (rough) cutting surface. It can be used on all kinds of metal and wood. A Nicholson is suggested. Cost: around $8.

A close cousin of a file is Stanley's line of Surform tools which are basically planes. They can be equipped with straight or round blades. Cost: around $9 for the straight type.

Glue Guns

Glue guns came onto the diy scene about 20 years ago, when I was toiling in the editorial vineyards of *Home Mechanix,* then known as *Mechanix Illustrated* (Ah, *sic transit gloria mundi!*). The glue gun burst on the scene, then more or less expired, because it had technical problems. It worked by melting and extruding hot-melt glue sticks, but sometimes the process was chaotic.

Today the method is reliable, and the tool is excellent for any quick gluing job—the extruded glue dries in 30 seconds—and it can also be used for caulking.

I like the Stanley-Parker line of glue guns. The GR 70 is good and so is the GR 60. The cheapest place, by far,

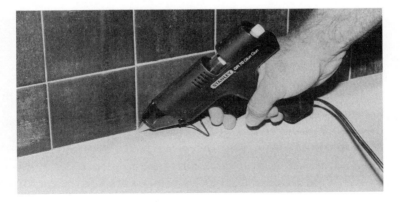

Stanley-Parker glue gun is very good. This is an increasingly popular tool.

to buy the guns is in K Mart. Last time I looked the GR 60 was on sale for around $10. I've seen it elsewhere for double that.

Also, buy glue sticks in bulk. K Mart sells 30 per package and is soon due to sell 40-stick packages. Stay away from glue sticks sold in crafts stores which are, typically, of poor quality.

Incidentally, if you need a *lot* of glue sticks you can buy them in 1000-stick packages from the Stanley-Parker Company in Worcester, Massachusetts, at a huge discount. Of course few diyers will have need for that much glue.

Hacksaws

These come in various qualities, including a tubular framed type which stores extra hacksaw blades, but you can get a perfectly serviceable one for $3 or $4. Great Neck is one manufacturer. If you want a hacksaw that will last forever, get a D handle model. The cost would be $15 to $18. The D handle's frame is made so that it protects the user's knuckles in case of a slip.

Hacksaw Blades

For around-the-home use, four types of blades are all that are really needed, as described by the number of teeth per inch (tpi). The more teeth, the smoother the cut. Hence, the following lineup: 18 tpi for moulding; 24 tpi for general use; 32 tpi for very fine cuts and 14 tpi for cutting wood.

Blades, of course, vary in quality. Blades labeled with the letters SS are the low end of the line and go for

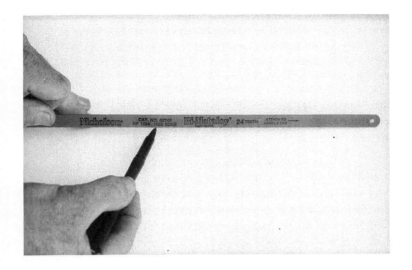

Good blades have the designation of HSS, for high-speed steel.

about 70 cents per. HSS, or high-speed steel, go for $1.79 to $1.89 each. These are made of flexible molybdenum. They last indefinitely and do a good job cutting threaded rod, angle iron and the like. They are a good buy, but they won't cut something like a heat-treated bolt.

The most expensive way to buy blades is one to the card. Either buy them loose or in bulk—they come 10 to the package (but you might be old before you get to use them all). Lennox is one good brand.

Thin hacksaw blades are also available for use with a coping saw where special cuts are required.

In terms of brand, I prefer Nicholson, followed by Stanley and Lennox.

Hammers

For around the house, the claw hammer, the type with the round striking end and turned-down nail-pulling section, is the most useful hammer to have. A 16-ounce weight is good, and you can expect to pay anywhere from $9 to $15. Stanley and Plumb are two reliable brands; I like Plumb best.

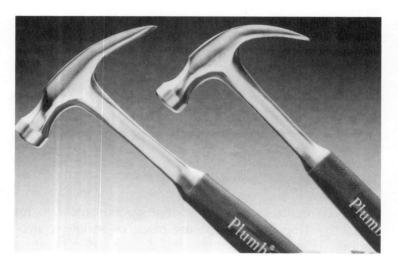

Good framing hammer, left, is made by Plumb and Enders. Claw hammer is at right. Suggested list price is $26 to $34.

Of course if you plan to use the hammer only occasionally, you can get a real cheapo for around $4 to $5. These are likely to have the words "drop forged" imprinted on them, as if this were an asset. It isn't: drop forging creates a metal that is brittle—not a desirable feature in a hammer.

A framing hammer is another good tool to have. This has a striking surface and straight claw, good for slipping between framing members to pry them apart.

One recommended brand is the Eswing, which has an all-steel form from head to handle. Plumb is good, too. The average cost is $26.

Hatchets

Hatchets come in various sizes and with a variety of heads. For around the home, a half hatchet, so called because only one side of the tool has a cutting surface, will serve well. The 3⅝" size (which refers to the overall size of the tool's head) is recommended. Cost: $24.

Levels

A level is a most important tool to have, and you want to make sure you have one that works.

M & D makes good levels, and they have the advantage of being the only manufacturer (that I know of) that has replacement bubble vials. You just screw the new bubble vial in place if you break it, and therefore you don't have to discard the tool. (Incidentally, if a bubble is off, most levels can be reset if they're sent back to the factory.)

M & D makes aluminum levels and, although they're

expensive, you might want to opt for one. Perhaps the best buy of all, though, is the American brand level. These normally sell for around $60 but they're on sale three times a year and go for about $50.

Miter Boxes

The miter box is used to guide a saw to the cutline so that the user can make angled cuts. A wide variety are available, but for home use I recommend one made of rock maple wood; these sell for around $6.95 and will work very well. (Recently I saw a plastic Stanley miter box for around $16 in a local Caldor store; you can pay $20 to $22 for a metal one. That's a lot of extra money to pay for something that's not needed.)

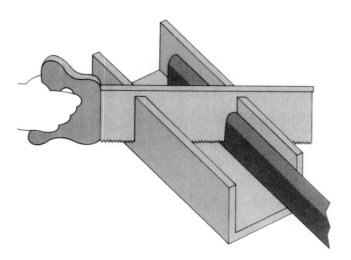

Wood miter box is just as good as others and costs much less—maybe $10 less, minimum.

Paintbrushes

Many grades of paintbrushes are available, but to some degree what you buy relates to how well you take care of tools. If you take good care of them, then by all means pay the money and get a high-quality brush. If they usually end up looking like a rock with a handle, then don't.

Whatever you do, don't buy a cheap brush for painting (or applying any finish) where smoothness counts. A low-quality brush just won't do the job. These brushes are fine for applying tar or epoxy or the like where the brush is going to be discarded after use, but that's about it.

FOAM BRUSHES

For one-shot use, foam brushes are an excellent buy. They can be used on exterior and interior trim of all kinds (including windows) and on small walls and ceilings, such as in a bathroom. They don't work well, however, on exterior oil-base paint.

You've probably seen them in hardware stores: small blocks of foam with chisel-cut edges and a short wood handle.

If you wish, you can clean them and use them again. My friend Dave Shannon has foam brushes that are over 10 years old.

Foam brushes come in a range of sizes, such as 1½", 2", 3" and wider; you'd choose the size the same way as you'd choose a bristle brush size.

Foam brushes are not going to make you poor, ranging in price from around 89 cents to $2.19. Quite a bargain.

Foam brushes. They work beautifully and cost peanuts.

If you are the kind of person who takes care of tools well, then by all means read on.

BRISTLE BRUSHES

Brushes in general are lumped under the heading bristle brushes, but technically this isn't an accurate description. Pure bristle brushes are those made with animal hair, such as that of a pig, and, in fact, are very expensive and only work well with oil-base paints. Try using a pure bristle brush with water-base paint (latex) and the bristles will become soggy and limp, just as a pig's hair does when wet. What manufacturers call bristle may be a blend of animal and synthetic hair, or pure synthetic, such as nylon.

What you should buy depends on what paint or

coating you're using. If you are using oil-base paint, varnish, or other now-water-thinned material, then I'd recommend the pure bristle brush.

You should go for quality. There are various ways to check for this, including observing the amount of bristles, flagged ends (split) and general bulk; thick brushes are better than thin. In this regard, if you examine various cheap and more expensive brushes you'll start noticing differences.

Still, perhaps the safest way to choose a quality brush is by price. I would suggest that you buy one 3″ brush (this can handle all trim and small walls and ceilings) costing anywhere from $12 to $18. Once you've spotted what you like, ask the dealer for a discount. When I was in a Sherwin-Williams Paint store I asked the dealer

The more you look, the more you'll be able to spot a quality paintbrush (on the left).

what kind of discount he could give me, and he offered 20 percent. Or, you can write down the brand name and call other stores to see if they have the same brush, and at what price.

If you plan to use the brush for latex as well as oil-base coatings, then you should get a synthetic bristle brush. The same quality criteria apply (flagged ends and bulk) and so does price: between $12 and $18 for a 3″ brush is about right.

Paint Rollers

Paint rollers actually consist of two components: the handle, which is the handle and the cage for the roller, and the roller itself. You can get rollers in various sizes, but the standard size is 9″ long.

In terms of a handle, get the birdcage kind. The roller is simply easier to slip on and off.

There are various kinds of rollers, but I think the following kinds are useful.

Mohair is a short nap roller used for applying varnish, polyurethane and enamel over broad areas, such as walls and ceilings in kitchens and baths. One complaint against it is that it leaves an "orange peel" texture, but this can be gotten around by first using the mohair, then following immediately with the brush to smooth it out.

For walls and ceilings you can use a 9″ roller with a nap of Dynel or some other synthetic fabric. Since this can get to be complicated, I would use price as a criteria. A good roller costs around $4, but if you clean it properly you can use it for years and the difference in ease of working and the finished job will be quite dramatic. If you want to paint a chain-link fence or

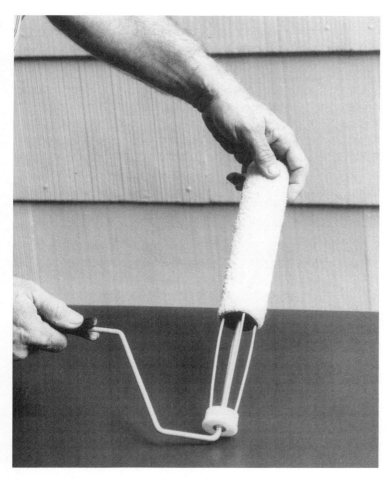

Cage-type roller handle is easiest to operate. You should expect to pay around $4 for a quality roller, but it will last a long time and work well.

---

rough surface, such as stucco or cement, a roller with a nap 1½" long is suggested. Again, buy quality. Average price here would be around $5.

One special alert: avoid those combo deals that offer

pan, roller and handle for $4 or so. They're invariably of poor quality.

One tip on using a roller: use a stick, which is a wood handle with a threaded end that can screw into the handle on the roller. Reason: you will be using two hands, which gives you better control and more strength.

Roller pans are available in either plastic or metal. You should get a good one with a deep well. My advice is to go for the plastic; you'll save money. For example, I recently saw a metal pan at a local hardware store for $2.98 and a plastic pan for only $2.29. Also, plastic pans are easier to clean than metal ones if you use latex paint.

Metal, left, and plastic roller tray. Plastic is cheaper and is easier to clean of latex paint. Here, the metal pan was $2.89, the plastic $2.29.

Paint Sprayers

If you want to do some serious spraying, my suggestion would be to rent the sprayer. The off-the-shelf sprayers I know of all lack the power to do a really first-class job. Only high-line rental equipment can do that.

There is, however, a device called a Jenni Can which can serve quite well. It consists of a canister to contain paint, a tube to disperse paint and a series of spray tips. An ordinary bicycle pump is used to pump in 15 to 20 pounds of air pressure. The air pressure then propels the paint.

The savings can be huge. The Jenni Can holds up to a pint of paint (or other coating). That's 16 ounces. It

Jenni Can. This can be pressurized with a bicycle pump and lets you spray paint very cheaply.

has to be cut two or three times with thinner to work. Let's say the paint costs $5. That would give you as much as 48 total ounces of paint for the cost of the paint (plus the cost of the Jenni Can [around $20] for a total of $25).

You'd even save money the first time you used it, assuming you used a pint, because if you bought regular spray cans at $4.89 to $7 you'd only get 7 to 11 ounces per can (the can is big but the actual paint content is not). To keep it simple, four 11-ounce cans at $7 would be 44 ounces of paint, for $28. For the Jenni Can you'd be getting 48 ounces, and save $3 in the bargain, the *first* time you used it. Thereafter you'd save more and more until ultimately the cost of the Jenni Can would be totally recouped and the savings would be large indeed.

Incidentally, the Jenni Can does a good job spraying car enamel, but here the paint must be used at full strength.

Planes

A 3½" block plane is all most do-it-yourselfers will require. It doesn't come cheap, costing around $35. Stanley and Handyman are two good brands. It can pay to shop around. This could be a particularly good situation in which to ask for a discount.

Incidentally, if you expect to be doing a lot of planing you might think about an electric plane. Makita makes a nice model for around $100, and, of course, this greatly simplifies the planing task.

Block plane from Stanley. It normally sells for around $45, but you can get it for $10 less if you try.

Pliers

Here, a couple of kinds will serve well.

One is the 6″ or 8″ slip joint. There are a couple of good ones. Crescent makes one for around $10, but Fuller has a perfectly adequate one for only $7.75.

Another recommended type is a 10″ or 12″ water pump pliers. This has a lot of power and can give you extra torque when needed.

Channelock's version of this tool is around $12, while Fuller's—perfectly adequate—is only $8.

Special tip: Fuller makes tools for other folks, and I

believe one of the big hardware store chains—Servistar—has Fuller tools under its own brand name.

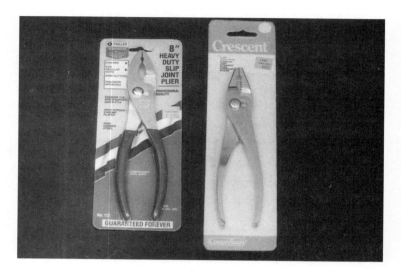

Fuller brand slip joint pliers at left cost $7.75, while Crescent at right was around $10—and all the diyer would require quality-wise is the Fuller. Note lifetime guarantee.

Rules and Tapes

There are a number of measuring tools the active do-it-yourselfer should have in his or her arsenal. One is a 25'-long tape with a 1"-wide blade. Blades also come ¾" wide, but when you extend a ¾" blade it does not maintain stiffness as a 1"-wide blade does, so fewer one-hand operations are possible. Two good brands are Stanley and Lufkin.

Be alert to sales on these tapes. Stanley has regular sales and Lufkin often will offer a free tape if you buy a quantity of another product, say paneling. Shopping around can yield quite dramatic results, as indicated above.

A 6″ folding ruler is also recommended. These are available in wood and in fiberglass; fiberglass costs more. Some people don't like the feel of fiberglass, and I agree. Two lengths are suggested: a 6-footer and an 8-footer. The 6-footer is good for plumbing applications while the 8-footer is good for carpentry, because most carpentry materials such as paneling, studs and Sheetrock

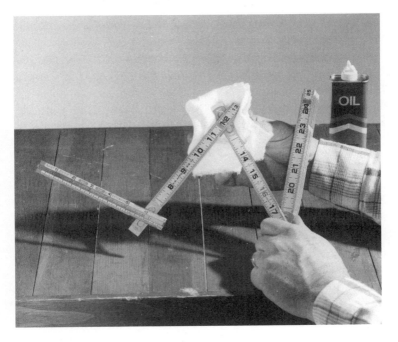

Eight-foot folding rule from Lufkin sells for around $18. You want extra good quality in rules.

come in 8-foot lengths. It's easy to lay the rule up against the item and know instantly how long it is.

To ensure accuracy, look for good quality. Lufkin regularly discounts its folding rulers in home centers. Cost for a 6-footer: $12. An 8-footer costs around $18.

Saws

Hand saws for cutting wood, despite the emergence of the portable power saw, are still an essential part of a diyer's tool kit.

For crosscutting—cutting across the grain—a 20"-long saw with 10 tpi (teeth per inch) will work well. For ripping—cutting with the grain of the wood—a 26-incher with 8 tpi is good.

Stanley makes good saws in the $12 to $20 range, but of course shopping around will get you an even better price.

Saws, by the way, are one of the items that can be kept going for years by resharpening them.

Scrapers

This is a tool which consists of a 3"-wide thin blade mounted in a handle. It is essential in interior paint jobs, not only for general wall and ceiling prep but for patching cracks and small holes.

Scrapers are available in a variety of grades, including ones with mirror-polished blades and riveted wood handles, but the key is flexibility: you can get a scraper for about $3 that will work well as long as the blade is flexible. Only this type of blade works well in applying patching material. If the blade is stiff, it's best not to buy it.

Crosscut saw. Stanley makes a good one.

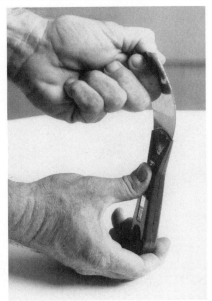

This is a cheap scraper ($3), but it's fine because it has the most important characteristic in patching: flexibility.

Screwdrivers

Screwdrivers come in a variety of sizes and tips—Phillips, standard, etc.—so if you buy an individual screwdriver for the specific screws to be turned, this can get expensive. It's better to buy a combination screwdriver, i.e., one that consists of a handle and interchangeable tips. Stanley makes one that will accept two sizes of Phillips heads and two sizes of standard heads. With this one tool you will be able to do 90 percent of the jobs around the house. Cost is $5.95 to $6.95.

Another screwdriver to have is the magnetic type, which holds the screws to the tip magnetically and is

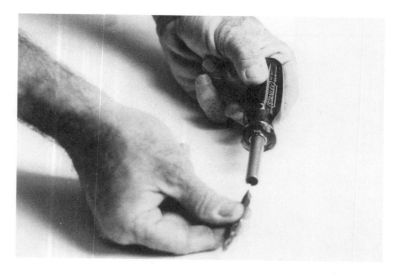

Combo screwdriver with two interchangeable tips (one is shown here) will handle 90 percent of the jobs around the house and save over buying a number of separate drivers of different sizes.

very handy when work space is cramped and you don't have enough room to hold the screw with your free hand. Bridgeport makes a good one that costs $4 to $6.

A screwdriver with a rubber grip is good for electrical work. If the screwdriver slips during the work and contacts live wires, you will be fully protected. A screwdriver with a number 8 tip should be sufficient. Fuller makes one that costs around $1.25.

Shop Aprons

Shop aprons are money savers because they protect clothing. I like the denim kind that covers the front of the body. Cost: around $16.

Soldering Guns

A number of these are available, but the pencil-tip, 140-watt gun from Weller is a good unit. I have seen it ranging in price from $12 to $25, so it emphatically pays to shop around.

Squares

Squares may be made of either aluminum or steel; aluminum is more expensive.

My choice is steel. Though heavier than aluminum (a factor which may count when holding it above one's head), it doesn't get scratched like aluminum does, making the markings difficult to read. Two manufacturers of good, medium-priced squares are Stanley and Handyman. Average cost: $9 to $12. If you want a better square—which really isn't necessary for occasional use—you can expect to pay around $20. At its high end Stanley makes a black level with numbers and markings in white.

Another good square to have is the speed square, which is an offbeat tool that acts as a guide for cutting wood at an angle; it also has markings to help one calculate and cut rafters. It's faster to use than a regular square, hence its name. Cost for a 7″ speed square: metal, $12; plastic, $4. Get the plastic and save eight bucks.

Staple Gun

This tool is very handy for installing acoustical ceiling tile, insulation and myriad other jobs. Staples are loaded into the gun and the handle is squeezed to fire it.

The way to save money on a staple gun is to buy one that uses standard size staples. Reason: hardware and other stores will sometimes run sales on standard staples and you can pick them up for a good price. This would not be true for offbeat sizes. Staple guns are also sometimes on sale.

Three brands of staple gun are common: Stanley-Parker, Arrow, and Bostich. I like the S-P, which goes for around $22.00. Bostich is high, around $32.00. Staples normally run $2 plus but sales prices are usually around $1.60. This may sound like a small amount to save, but staples can be gobbled up at a very quick rate and the pennies can add up so you want to be able to buy staples that are competitively priced.

Stud Finder

This is for finding studs behind walls. There are various kinds, but the one I like is made by Sears and is electronic. It is drawn along the wall and measures the difference in density behind the wall. The Sears catalog lists it for $9.64, but it does go on sale every now and then for considerably less. Sales are usually held just before the autumn.

T Bevels

The T bevel is used in cutting rafters and other framing members. It comes in a number of styles and prices, including rosewood and metal—but one with a plastic handle and nickel-plated blade is suggested. The version costs around $5, a far cry from what you'd pay for

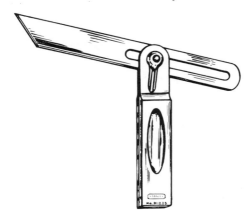

T bevel. You can get one of rosewood and metal for around $20 but the plastic one (from Stanley) shown here costs around $5. I recently saw one in the Harbor Freight catalog for $2.65.

rosewood—say $20. I saw a T bevel in the Harbor Freight catalog for $2.65.

Tin Snips

For some reason, a lot of junk tin snips are on the market, so I think it is important to stay with what definitely works.

Wiss makes very good snips. For intricate cutting, get what is known as aviation snips (models for cutting both left and right are made). These cost around $13. For straight cuts, get the standard snips. These go for about $19. The nice feature they offer is a slightly toothed blade that grips the metal being cut and tends to keep the cut straight.

Torches, Propane

Here, I would stick to the Turner or Bernzomatic brand names. The reason is that when you need replacement parts such as a tip, replacement orifice or gas they'll be easier to find than an off brand. The torch comes with a needle tip which is useful in soldering and many other tasks. You can save a bit by buying the Turner brand. Cost: around $12.

Utility Knives

This tool is good for cutting everything from carpeting to Sheetrock. It comes in a couple of different models. One type has a push-pull blade, while the other is permanently affixed.

You can't cut corners on snips. Only good ones are called for, and Wiss makes good ones.

I don't like the push-pull type, it's inconvenient. Better, I think, is to invest in a small holster and sheathe the knife in it. When needed, it can easily be pulled out.

Utility knives come with regular and heavy-duty blades.

Regular will be fine. Stanley makes a good utility knife. Figure around $2.40 for the knife and $2 for the holster.

Vise

You can pay a lot of money for an excellent vise, such as the ones Columbia makes, but I think a low-cost vise can be used with perfectly good results. I bought a 4" utility vise from the Harbor Freight catalog for $19 and it works very well. Fuller also makes good, low-cost vises.

I also got a very solid vise for virtually nothing at a garage sale.

Vise Grip Pliers

This is the main brand name of a locking grip pliers, a wonderful tool. It can be used as a straight pliers, but it's big advantage is that it can be clamped tightly on an object and then turned. This allows the user to put a great deal more pressure on the item.

Locking pliers come in various sizes and in different brands, including the original Vise Grips. In my view, the original brand is still the best, and you should shop around on a bargain for them. They come with smooth as well as serrated jaws and in various sizes. I suggest the 7"-long model. It goes for around $11 or $12.

Wrenches

There are a number of different wrenches that it would be helpful to have around.

One such is the pipe wrench. I recently saw a set of

four in the Harbor Freight catalog for around $14, but although the price is right, I don't think the average person will need that many. If you don't have any pipe wrenches I would start by getting a 10″ wrench and maybe a 14″ (the jaws go wider as the wrench gets longer). This should serve you well in almost any conceivable situation.

Ridgid is top-of-the-line on pipe wrenches, but I would stick with Fuller. Average cost of a 10″ Fuller pipe wrench would be $8.95 while Ridgid would be almost twice that: $14.95. Like Ridgid, Fuller carries a lifetime guarantee.

Another important wrench is the adjustable open-end type, which has flat jaws and a chrome head and handle. This wrench has become synonymous with the brand name Crescent, which is top-of-the-line; Fuller makes one for about half the price of a Crescent.

I would suggest a Fuller, 10″ long. Cost: under $10.

POWER TOOLS

Like hand tools, power tools come in gradations of quality, and there are quite a few types available. For the active do-it-yourselfer, though, I think there are only a few that are truly useful.

Circular Saws

This is the tool used for cutting and ripping boards and manufactured wood products of all kinds. Various kinds are available, ranging from high-powered types to ones that are very ordinary.

For the diyer, a 7¼″ Skil saw costing around $60 to $65 is a good bet. Catalogs carry them at better prices than just about anyone so these are the prices I'm thinking of. You may do better in stores but I doubt it.

In terms of blades, a combination blade ($10), a plywood cutting blade ($12) and a carbide toothed blade for around $16 should serve you well.

Circular saw. Model shown from Skil goes for around $65.

Electric Drills

Here, the Black and Decker drill (³⁄₈″) is recommended. The model that goes for around $40 is good, and they also make one for around $65 but the less expensive model will be fine.

A wide variety of accessories is available, from drill bits of varying kinds to sanding wheels and screwdriver bits. I would say a screwdriver bit, reamer bit and some speed bores of ⅝″, ¾″ and 1″ will handle just about any job you have.

Saber Saws

For making intricate cuts in wood, such as curves and sharp angles, the saber saw is a must. Its thin, vertically moving blade makes this possible.

Here, the Black and Decker variable speed saber saw should work out well. Varying the trigger pressure allows the blade to cut more slowly or quickly. Cost is around $119. Periodically, by the way, Black and Decker offers rebates.

Next up the line in quality would be Skil, and above that are the Porter cable and Bosch saws. But, as mentioned, for around-the-home use the B & D will work out well.

Look for nests of blades on sale. Cost is around $13.

Sanders

For sanding I like Makita's palm sander (around $59), which I've seen for $49 and which whacks along at 11,000 rpms.

B & D also makes a good oscillating sander. If you need a belt sander you can always rent it.

Screw Guns

The cordless screw gun is here to stay. It makes driving screws a piece of cake.

Skil makes an $89 cordless screw gun that is quite good. While they make a $49 model I recommend the higher-priced one.

Makita makes a good gun for $59 or so.

Table Saws

The table saw is an excellent tool to have, particularly for ripping wood (cutting it lengthwise).

Here, price is a good criteria of value. The saw should cost between $200 and $260. If you pay less than $200 you have to start worrying about the quality of the saw.

RENTAL SHOPS

Sometimes it can pay to rent a tool rather than buy it, particularly if you have a specialized need. Why buy a tool you're going to use once or twice, say, in 10 years?

Rental tools are also good when you need a lot of muscle. These tools are industrial strength and can do things their non-industrial-strength brothers can't do.

What types of tools are available, and for what jobs?

Let's put it this way: just about everything you can imagine is available.

It's very important to shop around, since rental prices on tools can vary hugely, up to 50 percent. Here, rental dealers expect you to ask the price and will be happy to furnish it. So use your phone and your Yellow Pages.

Also:

If you plan to use something for a long time, perhaps you can work out cheaper rates than you'd normally pay.

Have the work set up before you rent the tool. You want to make sure you use the tool for every minute you pay for.

If it's an outdoor job, make sure you can use the tool when you rent it.

If you figure on purchasing a tool, it sometimes pays to try a rental unit out first. It can quickly tell you if the tool's for you.

Incidentally, make sure you know what you're renting. Many times there are extra charges, such as for drill bits, sawteeth wear, and so forth.

4

SAVING ON BUILDING MATERIALS AND PRODUCTS

Cabinets

Cabinets for the bath and kitchen are right up there with the most expensive items one can purchase, but you can also get them, as noted earlier in the book, at phenomenal discounts, simply because the markup is obscene and people are caught up in some kind of spell when it comes to cabinets. They forget that cabinets are just pretty boxes made of different materials and finished by craftsmen or machines.

Just how obscene are the prices? Listen to Nick DeRosa, professional furniture and cabinet finisher for the last 30 years.

"The distributor gets a base cabinet from the manufacturer for $150 and then charges $500 for it. The markup is much more than 100 percent."

Before deciding what you should buy, you should know something about cabinet quality. While this can get complicated, maybe what Nick, who has seen many a cabinet in his time, says is all you need to remember. He recommends that the cabinet should be mostly wood, either solid or plywood.

Kitchen cabinets come in three basic types. Stock cabinets refer to those that are built in set sizes in 3" increments, ranging from 12" to 48" wide. The cabinets that hang on the wall—called, not surprisingly, hangers—usually come 12" deep, and base cabinets—those that rest on the floor—come 24" deep. They come in various heights, but height, as shall be detailed later, is not the most critical consideration in buying.

Another cabinet is a semi-custom type. Various manufacturers keep the cabinet sizes they have available in their catalogs, and you pick what you want.

Custom cabinets are built to fit the existing space.

All cabinets are built in two different styles: European, with "frameless" fronts, and American "framed," which have a frame into which the door closes. The Euro style allows much more space in the front.

Of the three kinds of cabinets, custom is by far the most expensive and is priced up to two and three times higher than the others.

If you can buy cabinets to fit the space available with stock cabinets, you can save much, but since stock cabinets are made in 3" incremental widths this may not be possible. For example, if you had 8' 4" inches of space to fill and the best combination of sizes of stock cabinets was 8' 3", you'd lose 1" (a filler board would be used to cover the space). With custom cabinets, all of that space would be available.

Is it worth the extra cost for the extra space? I doubt it. How many people fill all of their cabinets 100 percent?

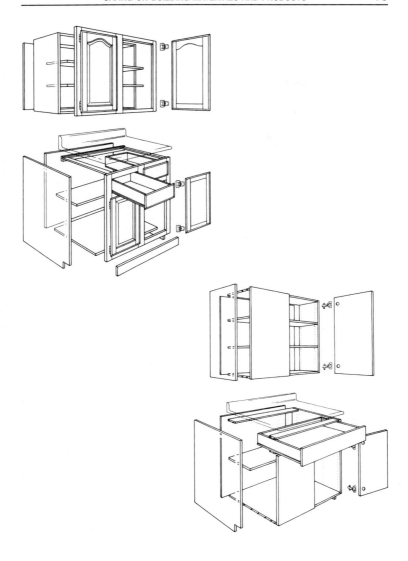

Framed and frameless cabinets. Frameless have no front framing pieces and therefore provide a bit more room.

Just how important are a few extra inches here and there?

Kitchen cabinets are made of three different materials: metal, plastic laminate-covered, or wood products and pure wood.

I don't like metal cabinets. Color selection and style are limited (Sears has some nice ones, though) and if one gets scratched or otherwise marred, you have a problem. Touching it up is a job for a guy like Nick DeRosa, and the people who can do this are becoming rarer.

I like wood cabinets, but there are quality considerations. Wood cabinets may be made of boards and a combination of boards and plywood or particleboard.

First, think of the cabinet as a box and ask yourself the question: how is the box put together?

A sign of quality is how the joints are made that join the box parts, particularly the front. If you see clips, you are looking at poor-quality construction. You should see either mortise and tendon joints (a tongue of wood fits into a slot), or doweled joints (box sections joined with wood pins) or rabbet joints (edges are cut to fit together).

Mortise and tenon joint, hallmark of a well-made cabinet.

If the cabinets are hangers, check the bottom to make sure they have substantial wood, such as plywood, not just thin (¼″) hardboard; the latter material is not strong enough to support hanging cups or other items.

If hangers or base cabinets are extra wide, check to see if they have reinforcing boards to keep them from bowing.

Also, the sides of cabinets should be ½″ plywood; they should not be made of boards, which can split. If hangers are more than 12″ deep they should also be ½″ plywood.

It doesn't matter if a cabinet has a back; some do, some don't.

Doors and front pieces may be boards or cabinet-grade plywood. It doesn't matter which. The more exotic the wood, the more you'll pay, although the exotic wood is just that and it won't make a stronger or better cabinet.

If it's hard to see how the cabinet is put together, ask the salesman to explain how it's made.

Even experts have trouble telling how a cabinet is finished. But it should have some finish, which is what protects the wood. No finish is an invitation to disaster and an indication that the manufacturer doesn't care about the cabinet.

Note that a favorite trick of some manufacturers is to sandwich some cheap wood product between good veneers of wood. These laminations are not the best and you should avoid them.

The main thing to find out about plastic laminate-covered cabinets is whether the cabinets are made of high-pressure or low-pressure laminate. Low-pressure indicates a poorly made cabinet.

All of the above may still not give you a good

indication of quality, but I think there is something that will: Visit cabinet outlets and look at the merchandise. Swing the doors, operate the drawers, feel the cabinets. Look. After a while, if you look at enough of them you'll start seeing differences. The wheat will emerge from the chaff.

Cabinets are sold by a variety of manufacturers, home centers, lumberyards, kitchen and bath showrooms, cabinet shops and custom cabinet makers. No matter whom you deal with, I think you should just remember how far up these things are marked, and take it from there. I would say that you should get at least 40 percent to 50 percent savings on stock and semi-custom, and maybe 30 percent to 40 percent on custom. Just shop around and ask.

Ceiling Tile/Panels

There are two kinds of ceiling tile materials: tile and panels. Standard tile is made either of wood fiber or soft insulation board, and it comes in various textured and colored surfaces including striated, pebbled, and fissured. You can also get it with a coating that makes it washable. Armstrong is the only manufacturer making 12″ × 12″ ceiling tile. The insulation board panels are made by three companies.

The quality of 12″ × 12″ tiles is usually uniform, but fire ratings are different—and are very important. Wood fiber naturally has a Class C rating, which is low on the scale and is not acceptable to many building departments without first being sprayed with a fire retardant substance.

Normally, tile is installed on furring strips, thin boards nailed to the ceiling to provide a level surface, but this is not required if the ceiling is wood. The tiles can be stapled or nailed directly to the wood, thereby saving the cost of the furring strips.

Much more popular than tile these days is the suspended ceiling, so called because it is suspended from the true ceiling of a room. A metal gridwork is hung from the ceiling and then the panels are laid into the gridwork.

Such a ceiling is excellent for hiding pipes, wires and the like in a basement, yet panels can be lifted out of the way for access.

Various materials are used to make the panels, including insulation board and plastic. The panels come in 2′ × 2′ or 2′ × 4′ sizes.

There is some misunderstanding about what ceiling tile or panels can do to impede sound leaving or entering a room. The answer is virtually nothing. What it *can* do is absorb sound *within* a room to make it less noisy.

Contractors have told me that Celotex is a good panel. Panels made of Styrofoam are not popular—they're too light, contractors say, and can actually blow out of the grid.

Grids, by the way, come in a variety of colors and styles and are sold separately from the panels.

You can save some money by shopping around for ceiling panels, but an excellent way to save 25 percent to 35 percent on the job is to have a grid that accommodates 2′ × 4′ panels rather than 2′ × 2′ panels. The latter uses up so much more grid that it adds significantly to the cost of the job.

Another way is to shop around for the grid. This can vary greatly in price, and you can get a better price if you shop.

Ceiling panels and grids are also periodically on sale.

Suspended ceiling from Celotex. This one, which uses 2' × 4' panels, costs around 35 percent less than those using 2' × 2' panels because the 2' × 4' uses fewer grid members to hang the ceiling.

Fall is a good time for sales, and so are January and February.

Cost of 12′ × 12′ tile (on furring strips) per square foot: $.40. Cost of 2′ × 4′ suspended ceiling, per square foot, including grid: $1.70.

Doors

Interior and exterior doors are made of wood, steel, and, of relatively recent vintage, fiberglass. It should be noted that including the standard door among do-it-yourself products is a challenge to do-it-yourself skills. A carpenter I knew with 20 years of experience once said to me that hanging a door still made his stomach gurgle. It ain't easy.

My friend was talking about wood doors, which are the most popular, and which are installed by degrees: the door is placed in the opening many times and is gradually trimmed down until it fits with the proper sliver of space all around.

Interior and entry doors differ in a number of ways. First, the parts of the exterior door are assembled with exterior glue, the interior with interior glue. Outside doors are usually 1¾″ thick; interior doors are usually 1⅜″. The extra thickness of exterior doors helps them resist warping.

For interior use, doors are usually the flush type: two smooth plywood panels are sandwiched over a core of either honeycombed paper or other pieces of plywood. The first is known as a hollow-core door, the latter a solid-core door.

The solid-core is far superior to the hollow-core type.

The plywood veneer, or panels, that act as the "bread" in the sandwich are usually made of luan or some other

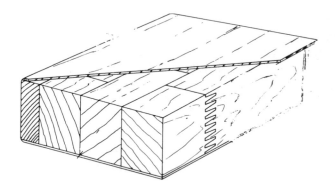

Cross section of a solid-core door. It consists of a sandwich of beautiful veneer with solid wood as filling.

cheap wood which is only suitable for painting, but birch, ash and oak—at higher prices, of course—which would be suitable for staining to allow the wood grain to show through, are also common.

Hollow-core doors can also come covered with a skin of hardboard, which is very low quality.

SASH (PANEL) DOORS

The sash door is composed of solid sections of wood; it gets the name "sash" from the fact that it is composed of parts. They come both 1¾″ and 1⅜″ thick, and in a wide variety of styles, and they may or may not include glass insert panels; or, as they say in the trade, "lights." The vast majority of sash doors are for exterior use.

Closet doors may be flush or sash and are simply smaller versions of interior flush and sash doors.

Sash or panel door. It gets its name from the fact that it's composed of parts like those used in making window sash.

Doors come with a warranty and this should be carefully observed. In some cases the door has to be painted immediately, or the warranty is void if, for example, the door warps.

PRE-HUNG DOORS

Pre-hung doors are also available. These come already hinged to the door frame, or jamb. All that the installer has to do is fit the frame into the rough opening in the wall—a considerably easier task than hanging the door in the frame.

Steel doors are also pre-hung.

STEEL DOORS

Steel connotes strength, and one might assume that there are few quality differences. Not true.

A steel door is composed of a sandwich of metal over some sort of insulation core, as detailed below.

The heavier the gauge of steel used, the better. This is normally 22, 24, and 26 gauge, with the lower the number the thicker the door. Good doors can be 24 gauge, but 22 is even better and 20 gauge is ready for a SWAT assault. (Don't laugh. Drug dealers in many cases install very good doors in their drug houses and reinforce them.)

When comparing doors, also ask about the interior. Manufacturers like to trumpet the energy savings one can achieve with a steel door, but this can vary greatly. Interiors may be Styrofoam or polyurethane; poly is better. And some manufacturers don't choose either: some doors are hollow, with no insulation at all, which automatically tells you about the door's quality—or lack thereof.

Some companies say the insulation in their doors is as high as R-15 (most walls have only R-11 or R-13), but this can be "snake oilish": the manufacturer will measure the R value "at the core" where insulation is thickest. The R value varies, depending on location, and the maker does not figure in the loss of insulation at windows—which are terrible energy wasters—to get an overall value. That is, if the manufacturer measured the R value at the window, it would be minuscule, and the overall R value would drop considerably. If you want to pursue energy savings, you can ask the store clerk for the manufacturer's energy data on a particular door. Average cost of a steel door is $185.

Pre-hung steel door. Pre-hung in the sense that it's already mounted in its framework, or jamb, and it then gets mounted in the rough opening in a house. Steel doors are made of different gauge metals, an important quality point.

WEATHER STRIPPING

I don't know of any steel door that doesn't come pre-hung. The reason: metal cannot be gradually trimmed to make the door fit into the frame; it has to fit to begin with. Therefore, steel doors come with weather strip already in place, and this is usually very good.

FIBERGLASS DOORS

These are designed to imitate fine wood, and the ones I've seen do a good job. For example, I've seen a light oak door in fiberglass that can be stained or painted and it would be difficult to tell the difference between it and real wood.

Manufacturers of fiberglass doors (and there are not that many) like to talk about R values of R-15, but this, as with steel doors, is "at the core," as they say; and windows will definitely lower the R factor.

Fiberglass doors come pre-hung in a metal frame. They are not cheap, costing about the price of a quality oak door.

SAVING MONEY

Doors are constantly on sale, and you should shop them as you would plywood and lumber; sales are that frequent. Remember, of course, to compare apples to apples.

When you buy a door, pay careful attention to warranty provisos. On a wood door you may be required to paint the edges (including the bottom edge) to keep moisture out; on a steel door you may have to prime it right away. If you don't, the warranty may be voided.

Doors do not normally come with locks, so figure this into your cost. Costs for doors run as follows: sash type, exterior, pine, around $370; flush, solid, exterior, birch, around $210; pre-hung, birch, $200; interior, hollow-core, mahogany, $78 (but lots less for pine and other woods).

Drywall

Years ago, if you wanted to build a room the interior wall and ceiling material would be plaster, or "wet" wall. A skilled craftsman (usually bowlegged and smoking a non-aromatic cigar never more than an inch long), would come into your home and apply a mixture of plaster and lime to a mesh or other base, smoothing it with a trowel.

Sheetrock, or drywall, is a much used commodity and always is on sale somewhere. I have seen it as low as $3 for a ½"-thick 4′ × 8′ sheet.

Plaster wall is still done, but today most walls and ceiling are made with drywall, also known as plasterboard, gypsum board, and, most commonly, Sheetrock (a brand name). It is composed mainly of gypsum, a powdered substance which is mixed with other materials and then rolled out in paper-covered sheets to various sizes. Standard drywall is available in 4' × 8' panels, and in thicknesses ranging from ¼" to ⅝". For walls and ceilings the ½" thickness is most commonly used; some people use ⅜" but this is simply too thin. The ¼" material is good as a lining when old walls are in very poor shape but you'd rather not tear them down; it's a big job.

Drywall is also available in "Type X," which is more fire resistant than the standard material. Type X is favored for use in garages because that's where most fires start.

Drywall is also available in decorative types in various colors and patterns. It has tapered edges, and to install it the edges are abutted and then the depressions or seams are filled with joint compound and drywall tape. The drywall itself may be screwed or nailed to the framing members.

Saving money on drywall is a simple proposition. Look for sales in the newspaper, then pop over and buy your supply. It could be better priced in home centers or lumberyards or building supply yards. You just have to look.

Normally, prices on 4' × 8' × ½" drywall run from $4.60 to $7.50.

You should stick to American brand names such as USG (Sheetrock) and Gold Bond. Although I haven't encountered any, I understand that some inferior material has been imported.

Like drywall, tape and joint cement for the panels is

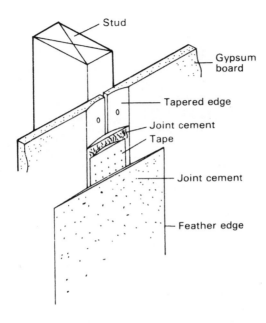

Stud

Gypsum board

Tapered edge

Joint cement

Tape

Joint cement

Feather edge

Diagram of a drywall seam. Good buys are always available on tape and joint compound.

also very competitively priced: you can get a five-gallon can for $6 or $7. On the other hand, it doesn't pay to buy too much because joint compound has a very short shelf life. You can end up throwing a lot of it away.

Drywall-like products that are even better than water-resistant drywall (which also exists) are Durock or Wonderboard. These cement-based products are impervious to water. They are excellent for use in the

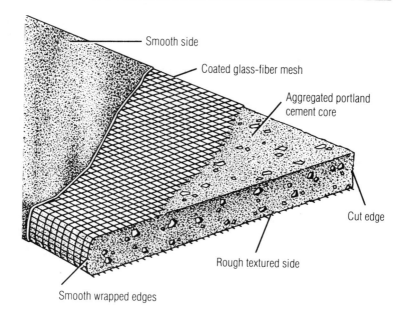

Smooth side

Coated glass-fiber mesh

Aggregated portland cement core

Cut edge

Rough textured side

Smooth wrapped edges

Durock, a cement-based product, costs only a little more than water-resistant drywall but is a must for use in bathrooms.

bathroom and cost only a little more than water-resistant drywall.

Exhaust Fans

The exhaust fan's main function is to lower humidity in the bathroom: the less water in the air, the longer the materials will last.

The government has certain guidelines about fans: the minimum accepted standard is the ability to change the air in a room at least eight times an hour. This is called cfm for cubic feet per minute, and fans do differ in their capacity to change the air. Of course the more capacity, the more you'll pay. For a regular 5' × 7' bathroom, a fan with a capacity of 50 cfm is adequate. For an 8' × 10' bathroom, a fan with almost double that—90 cfm—is acceptable, but 100 cfm is even better.

Exhaust fans, also called ventilating fans, make noise, and this is measured in units called "sones." The quieter the fan, the more you'll pay, so compare sones while shopping. One sone is about equal to the sound a refrigerator makes. You'd want to buy a fan with less than three sones.

Fans may or may not also have automatic controls, another extra of course. Automatic controls ultimately save money because when the light is put on the fan goes on automatically and when turned off the fan turns off, too.

An even better feature is a dehumidistat, which will turn the fan off automatically once the humidity gets to a certain level.

Two good brands are Broan and Nutone. Neither is cheap, being in the $150 to $250 range, but I've seen them for a lot less than that in home centers.

Fencing

Wooden fencing comes in a tremendous array of styles and is made of various materials. Usually, the closer one is to the source of the wood, the cheaper the fencing will be. For example, if you live in an area where black locust grows (such as the South) you will find black locust fencing inexpensive. If you live in northern California where redwood is plentiful, redwood fencing will carry a good price.

Two of the more popular materials for fencing are redwood and cedar. Both come in various grades based on appearance. You should look at whatever grades the dealer has and see if you can get a grade that costs the least to suit you. Neither cedar nor redwood has to be finished. Both will weather to a silvery gray color.

Lower in cost than cedar and redwood is pressure-treated wood. Typically, a local wood is treated with chemicals to make it insect-proof and rot-proof.

Fencing is frequently on sale, and you should shop around to get the best possible buy.

Finally, hot-dipped galvanized nails should be used in erecting fencing, and this can be expensive. Check the general hardware section for tips on saving on galvanized nails.

Flooring

The four most commonly used flooring materials in the home are wood, resilient flooring, ceramic tile, and carpeting.

WOOD

Wood flooring is hardwood which is tough enough to stand up to foot traffic. It comes in various grades, but these relate more to appearance than durability, and you definitely will pay more for the better appearance. The flooring is usually oak, birch, maple, or pecan.

Strip flooring is the most commonly available form of wood flooring. Strips are available in random lengths from 1″ to 3″ wide and ³⁄₈″ to 25/32″ thick with tongue and groove edges: grooves and tongues on boards fit together.

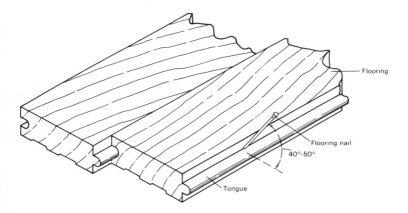

Strip flooring. This is clear or blemish free. Wood flooring is priced by appearance, and you can save if you buy flooring with what flooring folks call "character marks" (but what I call knots, dings, and mars).

A close cousin of strip flooring is plank flooring. This also comes with tongue and groove edges; the planks are usually 6″ to 7″ wide but may be as narrow as 3″. Plank flooring is often installed by being screwed to the floor; plugs are used to cover the screwheads and give an old-fashioned plug effect.

Parquet flooring refers to squares of wood which vary in size from 9″ to 36″; it also is assembled with tongue and groove edges.

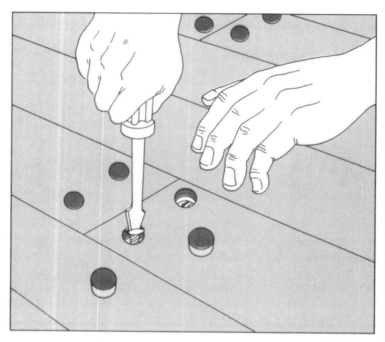

Plank flooring. It's expensive; shop around for best prices.

Flooring may come finished or unfinished (raw wood). Because of manufacturing methods, finished plank and strip floorings come with relatively wide grooves so the pieces aren't flush against one another. Otherwise, slight height differences among boards would be noticeable. If you do not like this, buy unfinished flooring. If the flooring is unfinished, it can be sanded and the board can be made flat.

Having to sand a floor adds to its cost if you have to rent the sanding machine and apply the finish. You'll also have to rent a nailing machine.

As mentioned, cost of the flooring relates to grades, which refer to the appearance of the wood. For example, oak, which is the most commonly used wood, comes in four grades. These are clear, which has few or no imperfections such as knots; select, which is basically clear with an imperfection here and there; and Common No. 1 and Common No. 2, which have varying degrees of imperfections.

Clear would be most expensive, select less, No. 1 less than that and No. 2 the lowest. Other hardwoods are similarly graded.

To save money on flooring, you first have to know what you are buying. The best bet, I think, is to find the flooring of one of the following brands, then compare prices. These companies are part of the Oak Flooring Institute and are set up to handle grievances, if any arise. The companies are: Partee, Plumline, Bradley, Razorback Robbins, Premier, Smith, Stuart, Harris & Tarkett, Tofco, and Smokey Mtn. They make various types of flooring.

Beware of companies that say their flooring is "all wood." It may be made of wood, but not of *solid* wood; it may be laminated or be made of lesser materials.

Beware of folks who call their parquet flooring, shown here, "all wood." It may be laminations, not solid hunks of wood. The best way to buy flooring is by brand names.

You should remember, too, that flooring is priced by *appearance*. You may find that you like a flooring riddled with knots and mars and are happy with its lower cost.

Costs: Clear pre-finished oak parquet, per square foot, is $3.08. Pre-finished oak planks are $4.10 per square foot. Strip oak, select grade, 25/32" by 2¼", is $2.75 per square foot.

RESILIENT FLOORING

This gets its name from the fact that it gives, or depresses a bit, when stepped on.

It comes in two forms: tile and sheet goods.

For the do-it-yourselfer, tile is the most popular material because it is easiest to install. Indeed, installing sheet flooring—which is installed in a single piece cut to size to fit the floor—is a very difficult job and should be approached with caution by a do-it-yourselfer. If a tile is cut wrong, all you lose is one tile; if sheet flooring is cut wrong, the job is ruined and many dollars are lost.

Years ago, tile was available in 9" squares, but now only one of the kinds available, asphalt tile, is made in that size. The other two types, vinyl and vinyl composition, are available only in 12" × 12" squares. I have also seen 3" × 36" tiles which simulate plank flooring quite well (Abitibi is the manufacturer).

Tiles may be the peel-and-stick variety or what pros call "dry back," i.e., the tile has no adhesive but is applied to a floor on which adhesive has been spread with a toothed trowel.

Tile comes in various thicknesses, and in no-wax or wax finishes.

Getting a quality tile that works for you may not be that easy. The anatomy of tile is too complicated to discuss at length. I would just say two things.

■ Stay away from imported tile (from China and Taiwan)
■ Stick with brand names but make sure that the tile you pick—you'll have to consult with the salesman—works in the area where you want to use it. One thing to remember is that tile doesn't wear as well as do sheet goods. It's questionable, in my mind, for high traffic areas.

Brand names I recommend are Armstrong, Kentile, Amtico, Nafco, and Tarkett. I would also recommend a close reading of the warranty.

Sheet flooring comes in two sizes—6' and 12' wide—and in whatever length you wish. It also comes in two qualities: inlaid and rotovinyl.

Inlaid is of far better quality. Whatever color or pattern it has runs all the way through the material. So if foot traffic wears down 1/16" inch of flooring, there's still much more color below. It won't wear out.

Rotovinyl is made of vinyl, but the wear layer is only on the surface, not all the way through as with inlaid. In some cases the rotovinyl has a urethane coating and in others it has a cushion backing, which helps it wear better.

Again, brand is a good thing to observe. Armstrong, Mannington, Tarkett, Congoleum, and Draco are good brands.

Read the warranty. The new Mannington Gold warranty, which covers their Gold line, says that the company will replace the flooring and provide free installation on the flooring for a year after it is bought. *That's* a warranty.

One way to save money on tiles and sheet flooring is to buy out-of-vogue patterns, just as you would with wallcovering. Savings can be substantial.

You can also shop around. Sometimes, also, you can

pick up a load of tile cheap at a salvage outlet. But be wary of what you're buying.

Mannington Gold sheet flooring. You can tell a lot about a product by reading the warranty before purchase. This one is guaranteed for a year—and would be replaced free by Mannington if something went wrong. *That's* a guarantee.

CERAMIC TILE

Since 1975, sales of ceramic tile in the United States have doubled, but it still is far behind some other countries (Italy is the leader) in producing tile. The reason for its surge is that the tile is now used in other areas—mostly the kitchen and living room—as well as the bathroom.

Ceramic tile comes in an array of forms and various grades, and its outstanding durability makes it one of the best cost-saving materials you can use in your home, assuming you keep it in place for many years.

The grades are standard, seconds, and thin decorative tile. Boxes are stamped according to the grade: blue for standard, yellow for seconds and orange for thin decorative tile.

Standard is the top grade. It describes tile that is perfect. Seconds describes tile that may have some surface imperfections, such as discoloration. Thin decorative is just that: thin and white and is usually only used on walls.

It's a good idea when buying to stay with American tile, such as American Olean, Wenczel, and Dal. Reason: they have all the trim parts you will need, something importers may not provide. (On the other hand, Richard Gibson, a buyer for Color Tile, a nationwide tile firm, says that he has imports and all the trim one needs. Color Tile, incidentally, says they will not be beat on price on resilient flooring or ceramic tile.)

I would definitely try them. Tile comes in everything from 4″ × 4″ tile to 12″ × 12″ which is used in living rooms and other large rooms.

CARPETING

In buying carpeting you have to be very careful to guard against rip-offs, because bad material can look good to the untrained eye.

Carpeting is made of five different materials. There are four synthetic fibers—nylon, acrylic, polyester, and polypropylene—and one natural fiber, wool.

Man hasn't beaten nature yet, and wool is considered to be the superior material. It is soft and luxurious and can keep its feel and look for a quarter century.

Next on the line of quality is nylon, which accounts for about 75 percent of the carpeting sold. It has one advantage over wool: it is more stain resistant, although almost all stains can be removed from wool if treated immediately.

Down the scale of quality are acrylic and polyester. These are not as stain resistant as nylon or wool, nor as resilient. Indeed, they are much more vulnerable to stains.

Lowest on the totem pole is polypropylene, which is mainly used as indoor-outdoor carpeting.

What a carpet is made of is only one indication of quality. One should also check how dense—thick—the fiber is. The more fiber the better the quality. To determine this, grasp the edge of the carpet and bend it back so the fibers spread. This is called "grinning" in the trade and it give you an idea, particularly when you compare one fiber to another, which ones have more fiber. The less backing or base material you see, the higher the quality of the carpet.

Manufacturers are slick in the way they can mount the fiber and make it seem a bit thicker than it is. Therefore, it's best to find out what the pile weight is per square yard. The more the better. If the weights are not printed on the label, you can ask your dealer what they are.

Placing padding under carpeting is a good idea because it increases durability by about 50 percent, which translates to a lot of money saved. However, just what is suitable for the particular type of carpeting can get a little complicated. My advice is to ask the dealer for a specific recommendation. If the padding is too thick or too thin it can make the carpet wear more quickly than it normally would.

Make sure that the carpet is installed according to the manufacturer's warranty. If it isn't, the warranty can be voided. You should get a warranty that guarantees against wear as well as manufacturers' defects. Also, look for a warranty that allows full replacement value, not one that goes down—is prorated—as time goes by. Most warranties are for five years, but some are for ten, which tells you a lot about what the manufacturer thinks of the carpet.

Comparing apples to apples is difficult when it comes to carpet, because there are so many private labels. My best suggestion is to shop for the carpet where you know they have good prices on other things. For example, if I were shopping for carpet I would probably go to The Home Depot because its prices are so good on everything else.

Garage Doors

Garage doors are made of five different materials: pure wood, hardboard and wood, metal, solid vinyl and fiberglass.

Pure wood is the best of the choices. It is made either of pine or redwood which is, of course, more expensive than pine, and it usually has relief designs carved in the panels.

Wood doors can be painted, but most people stain and apply a protective coating to allow the beauty of the wood to show through.

According to my friend Paul Sandburg, proprietor of Freelance Garage Doors in Northport, New York, such doors will cost an average of $300 off the shelf.

A little lower on the scale are wood doors with hardboard panels set in frames. The hardboard should be tempered; untempered hardboard will deteriorate in two or three years. These doors come raw and must be given a primer coat and two coats of finish paint immediately. If the door is nicked, exposing the hardboard to weather, it must be given a protective touch-up immediately.

Metal doors may be either molded metal or framed with steel. The molded type consists of a thin skin of metal over a core of insulation. Here, beware of the gauge of the metal. It can be thin, very low quality material to thicker high quality material.

Think twice about getting metal if there are kids around. If an errant baseball dents the door, the indentation cannot be taken out.

The other kind of metal door has a core of rigid insulation set into the frame; the insulation is visible on the back side of the door.

A money-saving consideration here is the good insulating property of this type of steel door. It does a much better insulating job than wood, and it works well in ranch-style homes or others where pipes are exposed to freezing.

You can buy metal doors in various styles but only two colors (at this writing, brown and white).

Vinyl garage doors are made of PVC, which is a very

tough plastic that is much stronger than the polyethylene used in the manufacture of vinyl siding. Like metal doors, the plastic doors come in various designs but only in brown or white, with most (80 percent) white.

The vinyl panels or sections are set in a metal framework. Room is left in the framework to allow for expansion and contraction, and the frame itself keeps the door weathertight.

Vinyl can take a licking and keep on ticking, as they say, so it is a good material to use if active kids are around. It can take a hard hit from a nine-year-old and not show it. It also is a good insulator.

The lightest garage door of all is the fiberglass door. In fact, light shows through it from the outside. It comes in a variety of colors, but because it is on the flimsy side many professional installers don't like it.

Manufacturers can make garage doors that are sows ears look like silk purses, and it's difficult for the unprofessional eye to see what's good and what's bad. Therefore, my suggestion is to stick with good manufacturers who make sturdy doors: they use thicker basic materials and better hardware. Three reliable brands are General Doors, Gadco, and Thermacore.

Most garage doors are heavy—150 pounds is not unusual—so even though they are opened and closed manually with spring and cables, the virtues of a garage door opener can be appreciated.

Prices on garage door openers vary. Some are down in the $100 plus range while others can cost $200 plus. Generally, it's best to go for the $200 plus units. But a very good—and low cost—opener we've come across is the one from Sears; it goes for about $149 (on sale) at this writing.

Gutters

Gutters come in five different materials: aluminum, vinyl, steel, wood, and copper, but not all gutters are created equal.

Aluminum is far and away the most popular material for gutters. It is available off the shelf, as it were, only in brown and white. It commonly comes 10 feet long and in 4″ and 5″ widths and different gauge metal, commonly .027 thickness; but even thinner gauges are available (.024). This gutter is known in the trade as "Reynolds Wrap."

I don't recommend 4″ wide gutter; its water-carrying capacity is nil. The 5″ is minimum (I understand in some areas of Florida tile roofs have 6″ gutter).

One way to get heavier-gauge gutter—.032, for example—is to go to a place that specializes in gutter and buy the length you need. You can get it up to 28 feet long. Lash an extension ladder to your car, then secure the gutter to it.

The other way (more expensive) is to buy seamless gutter. This also comes in .032 in white (it comes in .027 in colors). This is extruded on the site (they have a machine to do the job on a truck) to the exact length needed.

One other way to buy aluminum is in 10′ lengths. This is very cheap gutter but it has to be assembled, and it's a lot of work.

Wood gutter is made of fir and is available in lumberyards in lengths up to 50 feet. It is expensive material and weighs up to six times what aluminum does.

Copper is great for plumbing, but unless you have deep pockets and marvelous diy skills I'd stay away from it. It's very expensive and difficult to install. It comes in 10' lengths, and joints must be soldered together.

Galvanized steel gutter comes in various baked enamel finishes and in 10' and 20' lengths. It is around the same price as aluminum gutter.

Vinyl gutter is the cheapest gutter of all. The main complaint about it is the same about all pure vinyl products: it expands and contracts, and leaks can develop.

Gutter comes with various accessory pieces, leaders, downspouts and the like, which must be paid for separately from the gutter itself.

Costs, per foot: fir, $6.50; copper, $5; aluminum seamless, $1.60; vinyl, $1; steel, $1.60.

Insulation

During Jimmy Carter's presidency, saving energy was in vogue with a passion, and insulation was on many minds. That time has passed, but insulation should be recognized for what it still is: an important energy saver and, therefore, money saver. But before plunking down your hard-earned dollars you should understand how it works.

The basic consideration in evaluating *any* kind of insulation is the R factor, with the R standing for resistance; specifically, resistance to heat transmission. When warmed air contacts the insulation it is turned back, to whatever degree the R factor is.

The benefits can be seen. In the winter, the insulation in walls and ceilings turns the heat generated by the furnace back into the house. This means that the furnace doesn't have to work as hard as it would without insulation, which translates into money saved because less fuel is used.

The same thing applies in the summer where air conditioning is used. Heat trying to penetrate through walls and ceilings is turned back, and the house remains cooler and the air conditioning doesn't have to work as hard as it would without insulation, so fuel is saved.

Of course insulation's benefits do not just help on a short-term basis: they continue for years.

Granted the above, the higher the R factor the more effective the insulation is, and usually the colder the area the greater the R factor. In places like Minnesota and Wisconsin, where it's so cold that people store their car batteries in the house overnight in winter, insulation with R values of 38 are not unknown.

Insulation comes in various forms, and sometimes the thicker the material the higher the R factor. But some fairly thick material, 1″ foam boards for example, can be relatively thick and still have a very small R factor. So be sure to research the R factor.

Insulation comes in various forms, the most common being batts or blankets either 16″ or 24″ wide; these sizes are made to fit between wall studs and other framing members. Batts are 7 feet long and blankets are 100 feet. Both have a nailing lip on the sides which is handy for stapling the material to the framing members.

Batts may come unfaced, or faced or covered on one side with foil or a brown kraft paper. The latter acts as a vapor barrier, and its placement is important because warm air carries moisture and you don't want to trap moisture within the insulation. Hence, the vapor barrier is always placed facing the warm side of the house.

In some instances, though, such as insulation placed in the attic, a vapor barrier should not be used.

This is insulation that is kraft rather than foil faced. Kraft faced is cheaper than foil. The only thing that matters when buying insulation is the R factor, which by law must be displayed on the product.

Insulation in batt and blanket form is another of those highly competitive items and is, therefore, frequently on sale, particularly in the autumn before the heating season. Take a careful look at the prices, remembering to calculate things in terms of R factor and square footage. It can be tricky.

You can also save by buying insulation faced with kraft paper rather than foil. It's cheaper, but it loses nothing in the important R factor.

Other available forms of insulation include rigid board and loose fill.

There are four kinds available in rigid board: expanded and extruded polystyrene, polyurethane and polisocyanurate. R values are in the R-4 to R-7 range, and boards usually are about an inch or two thick and come in panels which may be $2' \times 8'$, $4' \times 8'$ and $4' \times 9'$. Again, they have to be costed out in terms of the R factor.

Some of these rigid insulations are designed to protect foundations, but they have to be suited for that. Extruded polystyrene can, but its expanded cousin, also known as Beadboard, should not be used.

When using any rigid plastic—and that's really what it is—insulation, note that building codes require that it be covered with at least a half inch of fireproof material, such as Type X drywall. This insulation burns and gives off toxic fumes. The purpose of the fire-resistant material is to keep it from burning as long as possible.

One other question—a big one—is whether or not to use rigid insulation. The R factors are low and you have to ask yourself whether it will yield enough payback in terms of fuel savings or be worth the expenditure up front.

Ask the local utility company what they recommend. If you live in Atlanta, Georgia, you don't want to buy the insulation needed to keep a log cabin in the Yukon warm and dry.

One other type of insulation is loose fill, so-called because it comes in chopped-up form that is meant to be poured in place from bags. Hence, the only place where this is feasible is in an attic with an open floor. It is also blown into uninsulated walls, usually by a professional.

Batt or blanket insulation is cheap, ranging from around 12 cents to 20 cents a foot.

Lumber

Lumber is graded, but one can get very frustrated trying to figure it all out. The system is complicated.

The best bet, I think, in terms of saving money is to approach any job with the understanding that it *is* graded. And as with plywood and other products, you want to pick something that is just good enough to do the job; you don't want the extra qualities of the wood to go to waste.

To help you avoid this forest of complicatedness, the following are suggestions for lumber to use on common jobs. Shop around. Wherever you see the lumber at the best price, by all means buy it. And if you purchase a couple hundred dollars worth of lumber at a lumberyard, ask for a discount—15 percent is not unlikely. If you are buying at a home center, ask for the sale price, and buy from whichever store is cheaper.

Studs are the vertical boards used in framing walls, and probably are the wood most commonly used by the do-it-yourselfer (and the contractor). I would use Stud grade (the word STUD should be marked on the boards) cypress, Douglas fir, western larch, or southern yellow pine. Lesser quality would be white fir, hemlock, white pine, and sugar pine in Stud grade.

Plates are the boards laid flat to which the studs are nailed (actually toenailed) when building a wall. Best here would be Standard or No. 2 Douglas fir, western larch, and southern yellow pine. Next down the line in the same grades would be cypress, white fir, hemlock, and redwood.

Sills are the pieces used on top of foundation walls. Use No. 2 or Standard cedar, cypress, and redwood for a top job. Western larch, Douglas fir, or southern yellow pine may also be used.

Rafters of No. 2 grade should be used, and the best woods to use are Douglas fir, western larch, and southern yellow pine. Cypress, eastern hemlock, redwood, and yellow poplar would be the second choice.

Joists are the members that are used to frame out a floor. The same choices for rafters apply here.

Note again that when buying lumber you should make sure when shopping around that you are comparing apples to apples. If you buy studs, make sure they have STUD stamped on them and all are the same wood.

There are a variety of other money savers, some related to buying, some to using the material:

■ Use 2 × 3s instead of 2 × 4s. Classically, 2 × 4s are used to frame out a house or an addition as well as other structures, but in the last 10 years or so there has been a movement toward using 2 × 3s in some instances, and of course these are a lot cheaper.

For framing out a basement, 2 × 3s work perfectly well. However, if you are going to insulate basement walls you might want to use 2 × 4s so you can get a greater R factor of insulation between them.

■ Space framing members 24″ apart. For many years, standard spacing for studs, rafters, joists, and other house framing members has been 16″ on centers 16″ apart. This was considered necessary for strength. Not true. The simple fact is that in most instances such framing is too strong—and represents a waste of lumber.

If you use this framing to build a house, the sheathing, or panels used over the framing, would have to be one thickness greater than normal. For example, if you used ⅝″ sheating then you'd use ¾″. But this extra cost still wouldn't outweigh the savings achieved by the wider spacing.

■ Buy common to get clear. Clear refers to lumber that has few if any knots or mars. Common refers to lumber that has knots and mars. If your project allows it, you can buy a lot of common-grade wood and saw out the good parts for your project, instead of buying clear grade to begin with. The price differential is so great that you can usually buy up to three times the amount of common lumber and still save. Common comes in Nos. 1, 2, and 3. The lower the number, the more you'll pay, and the fewer the knots and mars.

One way to save on buying clear lumber is to buy common grade and then cut out clear portions for your project. Clear costs 3 or 4 times what common costs, so even though you'll have a lot of waste you'll still do better than you would by buying only clear.

■ Use common as is. Another way to save is to use common lumber as is for your project, minimizing the mars by swabbing it with an antique or wood-grain finish. You should select the boards and make sure that they are not warped and the knots are tight. If the knots are loose, they can be glued in tight.

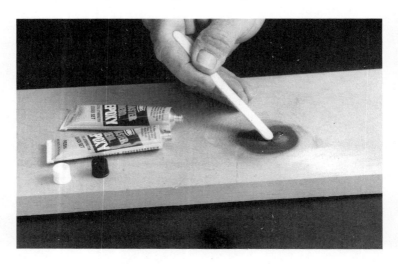

Cheap boards with loose knots can be revivified by gluing the knots tightly in place.

■ Reclaim warped boards. You may have some old boards lying around the house that are warped. Don't necessarily assume they are kaput. Set the board(s) on pairs of bricks, then pile other bricks on the convex side of the warp for a few days to take out the sag. It's a good idea to also wet the boards a bit before applying the weight.

Warped board can be straightened by weighing down the warped part for a few days. Wet the board first.

Another way to remove a warp is to make partial saw cuts close together at the point of the warp. This will allow the board to bend back to straightness.

■ Use common lumber to make things. People automatically assume that if they want to make a fancy chair or some other looks-intensive item, expensive lumber such as oak, mahogany, or redwood must be used. Not so. Common lumber 2 × 4, 2 × 6 and 4 × 4 can be tooled quite nicely and, when finished, look quite good.

■ Create designs to minimize waste. When laying out a project—a table, for example—try to design it within the commonly available sizes of lumber so you don't have to cut the wood and end up with waste. For example, you wouldn't want to design a deck that is 15 feet wide. It's better to plan one that is 16 feet wide and be able to use the lumber sizes commonly available.

■ Buy lumber on sale for future use. If you see studs or the like on sale, by all means buy it and store it, as long as you can be sure that you will be able to use it. If it sits in a shed getting warped it's no bargain at all. The best way to store wood, incidentally, is to make sure it is tightly tied together and out of the sun.

Lumber for building decks is commonly either redwood, cedar, or pressure-treated, also known as CCA. What is available will depend on where you live.

Redwood and cedar comes in grades and can be very expensive, depending on the grade you buy.

Pressure-treated lumber, on the other hand, is relatively inexpensive. For standard board sizes, lattice, and posts, look for southern yellow pine with a .40 chemical content. Other species of wood can't touch this quality. Incidentally, before using pressure-treated (CCA) wood, you may want to research it a bit—there's controversy over its safeness. (Contact your local EPA office.)

One good way to save is to build the deck structure out of less expensive lumber, and use cedar or redwood, which is much prettier, for the decking and railing.

Lumber is sold by the lineal foot, and usually the longer the board the less you will pay. For example, if you needed a pair of 2 × 4s 8 feet long, you would save by buying a 16-footer and cutting the board in half.

Check the cut-up bin at the lumberyard. As with plywood, there may be pieces in the bin that are just the right size for your project.

If you're fortunate enough to live near a lumber mill, you may be able to get undressed—unfinished—lumber at perhaps 20 to 25 percent of what you'd pay for dressed lumber. This is not smooth material, but for outdoor sheds and the like it may work just fine.

You may have decided that you need a particular

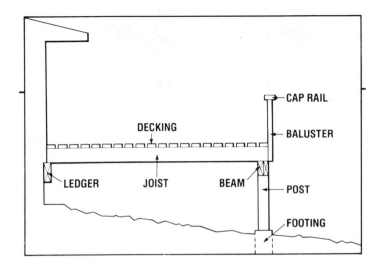

You can save 30 percent on outside lumber when making deck by building the supporting structure—whatever doesn't show—of cheap pressure-treated lumber and using cedar or the like for exposed parts.

grade of lumber for a project, say No. 1 common. But before you start the job, look at the next lower grade. You may decide it's okay and save that much more. In fact, before you work up your project it would be a good idea to visit a lumberyard and find out what's available and what it looks like.

Buy salvage lumber. This is lumber that has been recovered from a demolished building. Contact people who know contractors who are involved in big home improvement jobs. Sometimes the contractor will tear down one structure to build a bigger one, and he may let you haul away the lumber for a small amount of money—or for nothing.

Another source of used lumber is demolition contractors. I would suggest checking your Yellow Pages and calling contractors in your area. The same thing may apply: you can get the stuff for practically nothing—or for nothing.

Other possible sources are farmers who are tearing down buildings, and other homeowners. Once you start thinking used lumber, you may be surprised at where a supply can come from.

You should take care before using used lumber, though. You want to be sure of what you are dealing with. Examine it carefully for damage, hidden nails, knots and the like. Boards may also be dry and brittle with age. One way to determine this is to prop the board up at one end on stairs and then stand on it to see if it flexes or breaks.

Another tip: probe the board with an icepick to see if there is any hidden rot. A board that has rot can only be used for one thing: firewood.

Before using the material, it's also a good idea to measure it and see exactly what sizes you have. Over the years lumber has gradually decreased in size, and a nominal 2 × 4 may in fact be that, not the 1½ × 3½ it is now.

When handling the wood, take care to avoid splinters, since old wood tends to splinter much more than new. It's also a good idea not to saw through knots. In old woods, knots are particularly hard and can take their toll on sawblades.

Finally, don't forget to shop around. Lumber can vary greatly from yard to yard and from home center to home center. Savings can add up quickly. Here, particularly, checking ads and fliers can be useful. Lumber is always on sale at one place or another.

Manufactured Wood Panels

Manufactured wood panels are panels made from scrap wood (or sawdust) and glued and bonded together under high pressure.

PARTICLEBOARD

This is the manufactured wood panel. It comes in various thicknesses and densities. Thicknesses are $\frac{3}{8}''$, $\frac{1}{2}''$ and $\frac{3}{4}''$ and in 4' x 8' sheets; it also comes 2 x 4 and 4 x 4.

Particleboard is tough and can be used for building a number of things. It is the standard material for countertops. It is also good for shelving. Indeed, it is packaged as shelving, and the prices are out of sight. Do yourself a big money-saving favor and cut your own, or have the lumberyard cut it.

Particleboard. With certain limits it's a good product—and it costs half as much as plywood.

Particleboard costs *half* of what plywood does, but it's hell on sawblades (a high-quality carbide blade must be used) and it won't accept fasteners in the edges. Also, it's very heavy. On the other hand, if painted or covered (it must be protected from water) it works out quite nicely not only for building things but as underlayment for flooring.

The smaller sizes can be handy for smaller projects and you won't have the waste generated by having to buy 4' x 8' sheets.

HARDBOARD

Hardboard is another of the old standbys, a thin, hard brownish material that comes in sheets of various sizes, usually 4' x 8' but also 4' x 10', 4' x 12' long and in smaller sizes like 2' x 4', 4' x 4' and in ⅛" and ¼" thicknesses.

Hardboard comes with one or both sides smooth, tempered, or untempered.

Hardboard costs about the same as particleboard and can be used in many situations, chiefly as an underlayment. But you have to be sure the manufacturer permits it. In some cases, such as ceramic tile, tile makers suggest a base or underlayment of plywood.

WAFERBOARD

This product is made from wafer-like wood chips, hence the name.

It comes in various sizes, but mainly 4' x 8' panels. In the ⁷⁄₁₆" thickness it's very useful as an underlayment, particularly for carpet, where its relative softness is an asset.

It can also be used as an underlayment for resilient

flooring just as ¼" Masonite (hardboard) is used. Indeed, you should use whatever is cheaper.

Waferboard can also be used as roof decking in the ½" and ¾" thicknesses. Waferboard is water absorbent, but once protected by tarpaper and roofing, it doesn't have any problems. It can also be used on exterior walls as sheathing.

The three panels above all go for $10 to $11 per 4' x 8' sheet. All you have to determine is which to use in a particular situation.

Masonry

Masonry is a term used to describe a trade which involves a wide variety of products, from brick to stone. For the diyer, the two most popular materials are brick and flagstone.

Other than concrete, brick is the most common masonry material. It comes a variety of ways. The standard size for brick is 4" wide, 8" long and 2½" thick. Most brick is red, but it can also be obtained in black, tan, white, and other colors, and the shades vary greatly. It is made with or without a glaze, and special types of brick can also be purchased for paving.

Brick with a deep red color is characterized as being "well burned," and is more durable—or higher quality—than brick that is pinkish.

Used brick is also available, but this may be more costly than new brick. In order to get used brick ready for market it has to be cleaned of all mortar remnants, and this involves labor, which translates into extra cost. Used paving brick, which might have had tar on it, is extremely costly.

If you are involved in a fairly substantial job, by all

means buy the brick all at once. Brick color may not be consistent from batch to batch. Different shades of color may be a sore thumb on a project.

To save a bit (maybe 10 percent), try prices at a few brickyards.

One way to save money on a brick patio is to lay it in a base of sand rather than cement. This saves money and labor.

Another way is to use a straight rather than diagonal brick pattern in designing a patio. Diagonal patterns result in more waste. Also, lay out the patio (or walkway) to accommodate brick size. If you have to cut a lot of brick, that means more work and waste. Design the project in such a way that, to as great a degree as possible, only whole bricks are used.

Flagstone is a natural stone that has been trimmed so that it can be laid as outdoor or indoor flooring. It comes in various shapes ranging from free-form to rectangles and in a variety of soft colors, such as yellow, green, brown, gray, and red. It ranges from ½" to 2" thick.

As with brick, one way to save money is to build a patio floor with flags on sand rather than flags set in cement. As with brick, design the patio or walkway to accommodate the size of the flagstone pieces. And do shop at a few yards for prices.

Molding

If you intend to paint molding, the so-called finger joint molding will be fine for the job. This is molding that is joined together with interlocking joints that resemble fingers. If stained, the joints would show and mar the

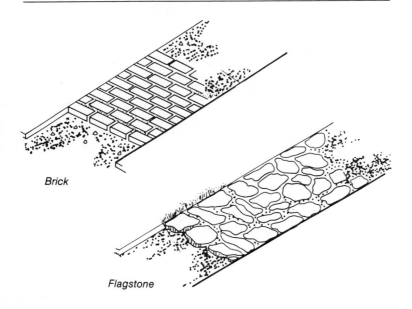

Brick

Flagstone

Here, both the brick and the flagstone walk have been built economically by keeping waste (cut) pieces to a minimum. Half bricks are used to fill in along the sides of the paving pattern.

job; when painted it doesn't matter. And you can save around 50 percent on the cost of clear molding.

Molding can be bought in 6' to 16' lengths, but it also can be purchased in bundles 3, 4, and 5 feet long. The shorter moldings cost less on a per foot basis; they can be one-half to two-thirds of the price of longer material.

Vinyl cove molding is another good buy, but you have to take care. It comes in two qualities, good and bad.

Finger joint molding is perfectly fine for painting and costs less than half of what clear costs (right).

The good stuff—it's all white—is firm and thick, and the bad stuff is flimsy.

White cove molding can be used anywhere in the house. It is secured with a special cement and is an easy do-it-yourself job.

Lumberyards and home centers often have a bin for pieces that have been cut off or damaged. Check it out. It may contain just what you need, and you'll save because it's almost always marked down.

Paneling

When it first came on the scene 25 or 30 years ago, wall paneling was extremely popular. It was used in bedrooms, living rooms, basements, all over the house—even in the bathroom.

Today, it is not nearly as popular as it once was, but it still is widely used.

As with so many other products, it comes in varying degrees of quality. Indeed, just a few years ago a Japanese panel came on the market that was so thin and was constructed of such volatile materials that it had the unusual characteristic of bursting into spontaneous flame on the wall.

No paneling around today is like that, happily enough.

Paneling is either 4 x 8s, or planks. Planks can be various widths and lengths as well as thicknesses, as discussed below.

The highest quality paneling is composed of a core of lumber sandwiched between veneers of beautiful wood and ¼" thick. While the quality of these panels remains the same, the cost rises steadily as the wood gets more and more exotic and rare. I have seen 4 x 8 rosewood panels that were selling for more than $100 each. That translates into thousands of dollars to panel a single room.

Still, the wood veneer used does not affect the quality of plywood paneling. The construction is the same, the face different.

Plywood paneling made like this comes, as mentioned, in 4 x 8 sheets ¼" thick. It may have a hardwood or softwood core; the latter is much easier to saw than hardwood.

Another type of plywood paneling does not have a veneer of actual wood but, rather, is covered with a vinyl which has been imprinted to look like wood. The back of the panel should have information telling you whether this is the case.

Another type of paneling is hardboard, also in 4 x 8

sheets with designs imprinted on the surface. These are available in a variety of colors and styles, a forest of which imitate wood.

Another type of 4 x 8 paneling is the fabric type (Plygms is one brand). Panels are covered with fabric (including the edges) and look like wallcovering or wood.

In terms of quality, hardboard is low on the list, though it's a perfectly good panel.

Plank paneling comes in various sizes from 3 to 12 inches and ½" to 1" thick (nominal or named size) and in lengths of 8, 10, 12 and 14 feet. The edges are tongue and groove, so as they are installed the panels fit together.

The cost of plank paneling varies according to appearance and thickness (also length and width). There are two grade ranges: the clearer the wood, the more you will pay. Knotty grades run from 1 common, which is the clearest, to 3 common. The çlear grades run from superior pine (the clearest) to D select.

Here, it would probably be worthwhile for you to visit a local paneling center if you have one in your area. These people specialize in paneling and buy in large quantities; many will transfer savings to the customer.

There are also sales to watch for.

Another way to save is to carefully plan the job so that you use as few panels as possible and waste is minimized. Check with the paneling dealer for some tips.

Also, you can use 2 x 3s to frame out a basement if that's what you're doing. These will cost much less than 2 x 4s. If you are going to be insulating, then use 2 x 4s.

Patio Doors

Patio doors can be considered windows, albeit large, sliding ones. They are made five different ways: pure vinyl, pure wood, vinyl-clad wood, aluminum-clad wood, and solid aluminum.

As explained in the windows section, wood doors with either aluminum or vinyl *cladding* are the best kinds you can get.

Patio door from Marvin, which makes aluminum-clad windows and doors in a rainbow of colors, unusual for the industry. Like windows, you can get a discount of up to 30 percent on this door, which would lop $270 off its $900 price tag.

Solid vinyl is subject to attack from ultraviolet rays of the sun, and can warp. Such doors vary in quality; some are very thin. Take care when thinking about buying one, since they can expand and contract depending on the weather.

Solid aluminum doors, like solid aluminum windows, are subject to severe attack by condensation. In cold weather the air seeps through the metal to the inside members where it condenses and does the damage any water does. Some makers included a thermal break material to prevent this condensation but it is not completely effective. Cost: $300.

Plastic Laminate

When it comes to covering countertops, plastic laminate is used—and this is a conservative estimate—more than 90 percent of the time. The reasons are simple: it's tough, stain-resistant, waterproof and easy to keep clean (some of the textured types are not so easy to maintain).

Plastic laminate is made by a few companies but is mainly known by one brand name: Formica. Wilsonart also has a large presence. The two control around 80 percent of the market. Micarta is another name.

"Mica," as they say in the trade, comes 2' wide and in lengths up to 16'. It comes in a wide array of colors and in several different textures. Usually the face is covered; the core is brown (actually it's paper: mica is made by adding resin to layers of paper and pressing it together). It costs about two-and-a-half times the cost of standard mica.

Plastic laminate comes in various thicknesses—and thickness counts. It comes in $\frac{1}{16}''$ (.0625) and $\frac{1}{32}''$ (.0325);

the $\frac{1}{16}''$ material is better. The thicker material is "high pressure" and is designed for use on countertops; the thinner material is only suitable for vertical applications.

In terms of solid core versus non-solid, the solid is worth considering. For one thing, when the edges are finished a thin brown joint line is not visible—just solid color—and the material never wears out, as the other will, because the color goes all the way through. There is no "wear layer" because the entire panel is a wear layer.

Sheet laminates range in price from 90 cents to around $1.50. Prices vary from outlet to outlet, and there are also sales sometimes.

Roll laminate is supposedly plastic laminate that is glued on like other laminates with contact cement. This stuff is garbage and should be avoided.

One other type of laminate—and I was stunned when I first saw it—was laminate already on the countertop. In other words, you get countertop with the laminate glued to it. All you have to do is cut it to fit in your kitchen and screw it to the base cabinets.

This material goes for $3 to $5 a foot (30" wide) and tends to come—at least the type I saw—in bland colors and patterns. It comes up to 16' long.

There is also peel and stick laminate. I am not that familiar with this, but you should know it's there.

As with wallcoverings and paneling, you can save on laminate by buying out-of-vogue colors and patterns and damaged pieces. You may be able to cut off the damaged portion and use the rest.

Plywood

For years, plywood has been a mainstay of not only contractors but do-it-yourselfers, although in certain instances it has been displaced, because of cost, by some other materials. Still, it is by no means less important than it has always been.

Plywood is composed of sheets of wood glued together; if interior glue is used, the plywood should only be used indoors (it is labeled INT). If exterior glue is used, then outdoors is fine. Quite often exterior plywood—which costs more—is used inside the house when it needn't be. The big key to saving money on plywood is to use the material that's just good enough for the job.

Plywood has two sides which carry letter labels signifying quality; i.e., the look of the plywood. For example if plywood has an "A" side it means that the plywood is free of knots and blemishes, as perfect as the manufacturer can make it. Its appearance is good enough for making kitchen cabinets.

On the other hand, if the side is labeled "D" it means the side is marred and has poor appearance. It still is perfectly usable in terms of structural quality, but it normally would not be used where appearance is a factor.

Grade B is one notch down the scale from A and grade C is lower than that. Following is a lineup of types and uses. It should be noted that before you decide what to use for your project, a stroll through a lumberyard or home center can be quite enlightening. You may decide, for example, that you can get by with a less attractive panel, and perhaps one that is thinner, and save money in the process. (The same thing can be done with lumber.)

Moreover, lumberyards and home centers do not carry everything, just what's available to them and what's popular. Of course, if you want something special you can have it ordered at special prices.

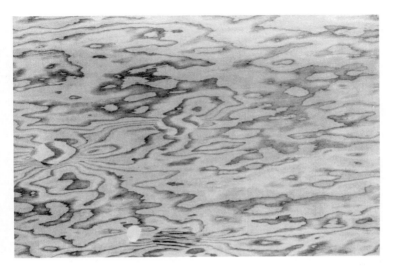

Grade A plywood. This is smooth, paintable plywood. While not designed for cabinet making, it can be naturally finished in some situations.

Grade B plywood. This grade has slight splits, and tight knots up to 1″ across the grain.

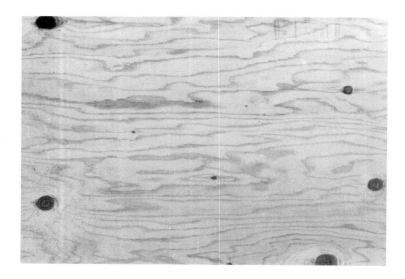

Grade C plywood has larger knots, discolorations and sanding defects but is still perfectly good material.

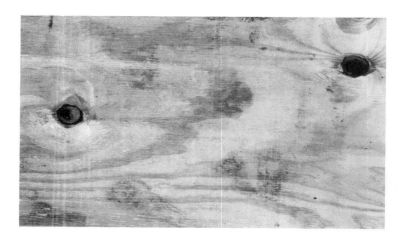

Grade D plywood contains knots and knotholes up to 2½". As you can see, as the grade gets lower the appearance declines and there are more knots and imperfections in the panel.

INTERIOR

A-D. For interior uses where appearance of only one side is important, such as paneling, built-ins, or cabinet shelving.

B-D. Utility panel with one smooth, paintable side. May be used for built-ins, utility shelving, or large cabinet backing.

Decorative B-D. This is plywood with a specially finished surface—striated, brushed, grooved, rough sawn—so the plywood can be used as paneling, accent walls, counter facing and the like.

EXTERIOR

A-C. For use on siding, soffit, and fencing where appearance on only one side counts.

B-C. Outdoor utility panel with one smooth paintable side. Used as truck lining and containers.

One other grade that's useful is standard C-D, which comes in both interior and exterior types. It is used as underlayment for carpet and resilient flooring. It is also available for exterior use. The standard use is for sheathing (the base for siding), but it is also good for bathrooms, where its waterproofness serves well in the high-moisture environment.

Another useful type of plywood is that stamped "SHOP." Not all plywood makes it through the manufacturing procedure unscathed. And some is damaged while being hauled around the yard by forklifts. For whatever reasons, the end result is "reject" panels—panels that may be out of square (be slightly misshapen), have damaged corners, have sand-throughs (the surface is scoured) or be gouged. These are the panels stamped SHOP. Look for them or ask to see them. They'll save you a couple of dollars each if the damage doesn't interfere with the project at hand (you can cut it off as waste).

Sometimes, too, you can check the cut-up bin at the lumberyard where they dump cut-off pieces of plywood (as well as other lumber products) that may be big enough for your project. If the project is exterior, though, make sure that the plywood is an exterior type. The only way to tell this is to find the letters EXT stamped on the cut-off piece. If you can't make sure, you run a risk of using interior plywood for an exterior project, a disaster in the making.

You can also save by planning just how you are going to cut the 4' x 8' panels to minimize waste. To do this, cut out a piece of paper which is 4" x 8", and then mark and cut this up experimentally until you figure out the best cutting arrangement.

To minimize waste cutting plywood, use paper templates and then draw the outline onto the sheet of plywood. Shift the pieces of paper until the best cutting arrangement emerges.

Doing a dry run with paper is, in fact, a good idea for any kind of panel product. (My thanks for this tip to Rosario Capotosto, a quiet, old-fashioned kind of guy who happens to be the best woodworker I've ever met in my life.)

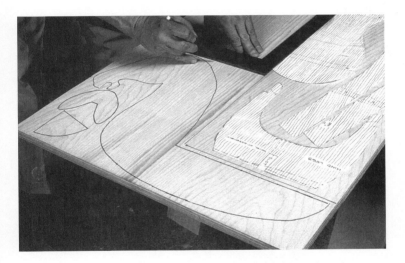

For best pattern cutting, make a paper or cardboard pattern of what you want, then lay it out on plywood.

One other tip: if you have a pattern to cut from plywood, make a paper pattern first, draw its outline on the sheet of plywood to minimize waste, then cut.

Like lumber, plywood is a highly competitive product, so make sure you pore over the ads before buying. Savings can be significant.

Finally, take care that the plywood you get has the

APA (American Plywood Association) stamp on it. Some people are selling import panels without regard for its manufacture, including not caring whether they use interior glue on what are said to be exterior panels.

Roofing

ASPHALT SHINGLES

Roofing comes in a variety of types, but far and away the most popular is asphalt shingles, which today mainly refers to fiberglass shingles.

Shingles are manufactured with a base of fiberglass

Tamko fiberglass roof shingles. Tamko got high marks from contractors. It costs around $20 a square (10 feet by 10 feet).

or organic felt if they are asphalt. In both cases the base is saturated with asphalt, and then ceramic mineral particles are applied to this.

Shingles can be purchased in various colors—white, black, green, red, and brown.

Shingles come 36" wide and 12" deep and with flaps or tabs. Usually there are dabs of adhesive under the tabs to keep the wind from lifting them.

Shingles come in varying grades. A few years ago, to determine grade, all you had to do was note the weight per square. A square means enough shingles to cover an area 10 feet by 10 feet (a square also consists of three bundles of shingles, each covering 33⅓ square feet). The heavier the shingle the better: 235 pound shingles (meaning the weight of a square was 235 pounds) were better than 220, which meant 220 pounds per square.

Today, probably because of the emergence of fiberglass shingles, which are lighter, weight is no longer a sign of grade.

These days, one key is the guarantee or warranty that the manufacturer assigns the shingles. Some asphalt shingles come with only a 15-year guarantee, but most shingles have at least 20 years.

Read the warranty carefully. Warranties are limited and also dictate which installation methods must be used. And the accent is on *must*. If the shingles are not installed according to the manufacturer's recommendation, then the warranty is void.

Incidentally, asphalt shingles—in fact all shingles—come with various fire ratings. A is the best, B is next and C is least, so don't assume that if you see "Class A" shingles advertised, as I recently did at The Home Depot, that it means the shingles are top quality. It just means they're tops in fire ratings.

There is debate about whether asphalt or fiberglass is better. It seems clear that fiberglass is better; that's the consensus of roofers.

As with most other things, though, you need more specific information to get a good shingle.

The best shingles around are the fiberglass shingles made by Owens Corning, Tamko, and Bird. They come in a variety of grades which means years of warranty but the 20-year guaranteed shingles are recommended over the 25-year shingles. Reason: it is highly likely that before 25 years is up you will want to change the roof, even if it is standing up beautifully. So why pay the extra money for the additional five years guaranteed when you won't benefit by it?

The profit margin on roofing shingles is not as great as on other products, but you can ask for a 10 percent to 15 percent discount and you'll probably get it. The average cost for 20-year fiberglass shingles would be 22 cents a square foot.

Another way to save is to check with dealers to see if they have shingles left over that are going out of style. They may not be suitable for the roof of the house, but maybe there is enough to cover a shed, gazebo, garage or the like. Don't forget to factor in waste of 10 percent. You don't want to be 95 percent finished with the job and run out.

ROLL ROOFING

Roll roofing is simply asphalt roofing in roll form, usually in lengths of 36 to 38 feet and weighing 40 to 90 pounds per roll. It comes with or without a granular surface and in different colors. It can be used as a primary roofing in some cases.

Owens Corning roofing is a shadow type. It is of a high grade and costs more than standard shingles.

Roll roofing.

CEDAR SHINGLES AND SHAKES

Cedar shingles are flat machine-cut cedar sections that are 16′ to 24′ long and resistant to decay. When new they're tan, and they weather to gray.

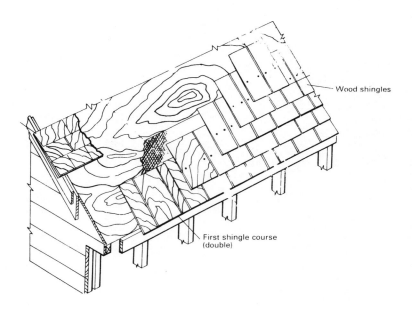

Machine-cut cedar shingle roofing.

Cedar comes in various grades which, like a number of other products, relate to appearance.

The top grades are No. 1 Blue Label and No. 2 Red Label. There are three or four grades below this; the appearance becomes rougher, with more blemishes, as you go.

The rough-hewn look in cedar is provided by shakes, which are cut by hand. Unlike machine-cut shingles, which are parallel on the sides and even along the bottom, shakes are uneven widths and lengths. Long thin shakes are less prone to warping than are wide thick ones. Also, heartwood shakes stand up to decay much better than do the others.

Of all the roofing products one can buy, however, cedar has the shortest life span—an average of 11 years. So it may not be the most economical purchase.

Additionally, it has a very poor fire rating. In fact, using cedar may raise your insurance rates. Check it out before buying. If the shingles are sprayed with a fire-retardant compound, they can get a fire rating of C, which is not fabulous but is passable. Costs: shingles, $1.30 per square foot; shakes, $1.

CLAY TILE

These are made of slate and tile that has been fired at very high temperatures. They usually come in earth tones but also are available in bright blue, red and other colors, and they are very expensive.

Clay tiles come in various shapes and are made to interlock. This is a job only for the very skilled do-it-yourselfer, and when the job is done the flashings—the metal material that seals the gaps in the seams in the roof—must also be installed correctly.

CONCRETE TILE

Concrete tile simulates clay tile quite effectively. As the name denotes, it is made of concrete. Unlike clay tile, it only comes unglazed.

The big difference is cost. It is only about half of what

clay tile costs. For example, clay Spanish tile would cost around $3.70 a square foot, while concrete tile only costs $1.25 per square foot.

SLATE

Slate is more expensive per square foot than any kind of roofing, but like so many other products it does come in a variety of grades, and in colors such as green-gray, maroon, and black, depending on the state it's from. Most slate comes from the northeast with Vermont and Maine generally considered the best sources.

Slate that is of good quality is characterized with strong, even color and straight grain. Lower-quality slates are coarse-grained and may have alien colors mixed in.

Cost of Vermont slate, per square foot: $4.60.

Siding

Some siding, such as aluminum, is not really suited to do-it-yourself jobs, so it is not presented here. On the other hand, there are types of siding that fall into the diyer province.

VINYL

It does take skill to hang vinyl siding well, but do-it-yourselfers do get involved with it.

All siding, no matter the type, is sold by the "square" (like roofing), meaning 100 square feet or a 10' by 10' area.

Remodelers like vinyl because it's a high profit item and a relatively easy job to do. It comes in light, flexible panels that are simple to cut.

Main pieces come in various widths and 12-foot lengths, and in various thicknesses, gauges, and colors. While there is no quality breakdown per se, vinyl siding can certainly be looked at in terms of quality.

In general, vinyl can be considered to fall in one of three groups. The lowest grade or group is the builder's grade, and this group is marked by siding that is available in a limited number of colors, chiefly white and gray but also cream and a sort of clay color.

One or two styles or textures are available, and it usually has a high-gloss finish. Characteristic of this group is the gauge of the panel, which is about .040 (very thin).

In the mid-range group you'll find a broader selection of colors (7 to 12) and a thicker gauge—.042 to .044 inches. The profiles are also much broader. The finish will also be less glossy than the builder's grade.

The highest quality group of vinyl siding is thicker than the mid range, comes in an even wider variety of colors and can have special designs and textures. It's finish is a low sheen.

In particular, gauge matters. If the vinyl is too thin, any siding beneath it, such as wood shingles, will tend to show through and yield an unattractive wavy look. Indeed, sometimes even the heavier gauges won't hide bumps or waves beneath, and it will be necessary to first level the siding before application.

Three manufacturers of siding that are highly visible are Georgia Pacific, Certainteed, and Royal Crest.

Royal Crest, which can be purchased at building supply yards, comes in three ranges: the bottom is "Journeyman," the middle "Royal Crest" and the best grade "Architectural." But the siding is so superior to others that its middle grade is better than the top grade of the others.

Prices for Royal Crest vinyl siding are around $44 per square for the lowest grade, $54 for Royal Crest, and $64 for the Architectural grade. Added to this must be trim pieces, which will, in general, bring the siding to around $130 per square. Like roofing, you can ask for—and expect to receive—a discount on vinyl siding of at least 10 percent and possibly 15 percent.

CEDAR SHINGLES

Perhaps second in popularity to vinyl siding is cedar. It is available in machine-cut form (shingles) and hand-cut form (shakes). The machine-cut shingles, which have a striated face, come in three grades: No. 1, No. 2, and No. 3 or undercourse. The latter is designed to be installed under No. 1 and No. 2 to lend bulk and a shadowy effect.

A close cousin of machine-cut shingles is the sawn type, which comes 18″ to 24″ long.

The shakes come with uneven butts (ends) and in various widths and thicknesses ranging all the way from ⅜″ to 1½″—and in some cases 2″ thick. They also come 18″ and 24″ long. Cost: about $1.35 for shingles, $1.80 for shakes.

PLYWOOD

Like standard plywood, plywood siding comes with veneers made of various woods, such as cedar, redwood, Douglas fir, and southern pine, and the veneers are a factor in the price. If the veneer is good-looking, the panel comes stained; if the wood doesn't have a good grain, then it is painted.

Also a factor in grades is the way the veneers are

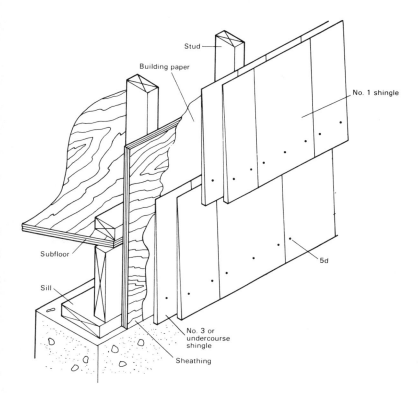

No. 1 Cedar shingles installed.

---

textured, anything from rough sawn to grooved. Thickness also matters. This can range from $1\frac{1}{32}''$, $\frac{3}{8}''$, $\frac{1}{2}''$, and $\frac{15}{32}''$ (this has to be specially ordered).

To ensure quality, look for the stamp of the American Plywood Association. This guarantees some quality. For example, some foreign manufacturers do not use exterior glue in making the panels, and this can lead to delamination (the coming apart of the layers).

Some of the panels can be installed with nails 24"
apart, which saves not only on nails but also on work.

Prices on plywood vary greatly, but generally it's around
a dollar per square foot.

OTHER SIDINGS

Still very much in the picture is real board siding. It is
made of cedar and comes in various thicknesses from
½" to ¾" and in widths of 4" to 12". Some board siding
has a rough side and a smooth side; the former is for
staining, the latter for painting. Profiles vary. Bevel or
clapboard siding is the classic.

Cost depends on wood and style. For redwood drop
siding, the cost would be around $1.90 per square foot.

Good buys on board siding are a little more difficult

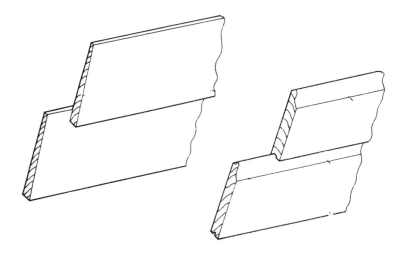

Board siding types. Lap, above, is still popular. In redwood it would cost around $1.90 per square foot.

to find than on other sidings because it is not a competitive product.

Skylights

Skylights come in glass and plastic. Glass is always flat, while plastic (acrylic) is always formed into a rounded, raised shape.

Venterama skylight. This 30″ by 45″ unit lists for *$480.00* but, as with patio doors and windows, you can get around 30 percent off.

In recent years, glass has become the more popular of the two, perhaps because people like its sleeker look.

Skylights may be movable or fixed, meaning that the glass or plastic may be openable or unopenable. In some cases the opening is done by hand or a pole, but there are also motorized units: a remote motor powers the skylight open or closed. Skylights that can be opened are also known as roof windows. It makes little sense, it seems to me, to get a skylight that is not movable. Hot air can build up at the ceiling; if the skylight is movable this air can be bled off. And on nice days a skylight can let in a lot of fresh air.

The sun can be a powerful force flowing through a skylight for hours during the day. To combat too much sun, you can get a skylight with shades, or, if you buy a glass skylight, one with low-E (low emissivity) glass. This latter term refers to glass that has been impregnated with a virtually invisible material that stops or impedes certain rays of the sun. It is said that low-E glass also lowers energy costs.

Skylights are susceptible to leaks. But on closer examination one sees in many cases that the skylight is not to blame; the number one problem is the way they are installed.

You can get a good skylight the same way you buy a window: by brand name. Four good brands are Venterama, Wasco Industries, Insula Dome, and Andersen.

You can save a lot on a skylight: most dealers I talked to said that 30 percent was their limit. If you figure an average cost of a skylight to be $400 to $500, the savings can be substantial.

Windows

There are a number of window types to consider, and huge discounts to be had.

PURE VINYL

Pure vinyl windows—which are made of varying thicknesses of vinyl—are much cheaper than other kinds of windows, but I would avoid them, even the ones that are obviously better made than others (those in which vinyl parts are thicker, for example). Reason: there's simply too much controversy about whether they're good or bad. Some contractors like them, but most don't. Some say the windows are intrinsically poorly made, while others are afraid of the fact that vinyl expands and contracts depending on the weather. This, the contractors say, eventually creates a gap in the framework around the window that allows drafts and water through.

Most manufacturers make vinyl windows only in white, though at least one is making wood-grained ones. Vinyl windows are easy to install; they basically drop into the existing framework. Indeed, they are a smaller window overall because of this. Manufacturers like them because they're high-profit: the contractor or dealer just gives the sizes of the window openings and the windows are quickly fabricated to the exact size needed from stock vinyl extrusions.

SOLID WOOD

These are available in various stock sizes in 2″ increments, and in varying qualities, ranging from what is known as "builder's quality" and "economy" (which is low-end quality) to high quality. Looking at the various qualities should give you an idea of what's better—and so will price.

Wood windows, it should be noted, have been largely supplanted by others (a friend of mine who works at a building supply yard says he hasn't sold one in six months—and it's a busy yard).

Wood windows come unpainted, so as the years go by you can paint them any color you wish. This is not possible with other types, at least not on the exterior side.

Vinyl windows can be dropped into the existing frame, as mentioned, but installing wood windows will involve removing some of the siding, then reinstalling it.

SOLID ALUMINUM

These are windows made in stock sizes of pure aluminum. Their big problem is that aluminum conducts cold, which leads to condensation on warmer surfaces and moisture which, in turn, leads to pitting. In some states, this may be less of a problem.

Some aluminum windows have an insulating type "thermal break" material with this but the effectiveness of this is questionable.

Aluminum comes in various colors and never has to be painted.

ALUMINUM-CLAD WOOD

This type of window is a completely different animal from pure aluminum: the core is wood with a thin skin of aluminum, and it does not have any of the condensation problems that pure aluminum has because the core is wood. Aluminum-clad windows are available in a wide variety of colors, and the cladding is only on the exterior of the window, which never has to be painted.

The inside is raw wood, which can be painted any color you wish.

VINYL CLAD

These windows are the same as aluminum-clad—the core is wood—but the cladding is vinyl. Unlike aluminum clad, they are normally only available in two colors—white and brown. Like aluminum clad, the inside face of these windows is wood, so you can paint it.

As suggested above, avoid vinyl windows. If you go for wood, go for quality. Look the windows over, try them, ask questions.

The best windows to get, in my view, are either vinyl or aluminum clad. Rather than getting lost in a forest of technical considerations, buy by brand names. Four goods ones are Andersen, Pella, Marvin, and Peachtree. These companies don't make degrees of quality. They only make one quality: good.

Within this context of selecting quality, and if you buy windows in stock sizes, enormous savings of up to 30–40 percent are possible. This translates into hundreds of dollars, even thousands of dollars saved. Hence, it's crucial to shop around.

Gather literature, visit home centers and places that specialize in windows (which probably have better prices to begin with), and ask for a discount. Haggle and discuss until you sense the dealer has reached his best discount.

Incidentally, windows come with double-insulated glass. If you live in downtown Broken Rifle, Alaska, consider getting triple glazing. Ultimately, the energy savings may be well worth it.

Corner section of an Andersen window, vinyl cladding outside, raw wood inside so you can paint it as you wish, and double insulated and with low-E glass. You can get up to 30 percent off on these windows. Standard double-hung retails for $180, for example, so 30 percent off that would be about $55. As you can see, if you order a lot of windows, this can add up.

You can also get them with what is known as low E, or low emissivity, glass, as mentioned elsewhere in the book. The glass is impregnated with an invisible material that helps cut down on the ultraviolet rays of the sun, the rays that cause colors on furniture, rugs and the like to fade.

OTHER WINDOWS

Seven or eight other styles of window are available, including casement (the kind that open vertically with a crank handle), fixed (they don't open), jalousie (movable glass slats), sliding windows (panels slide horizontally), hopper (aka bottom-hinged windows; the window swings down), awning (a single glass panel hinged at the top), and top-hinged (like awning windows except that they swing out at the top).

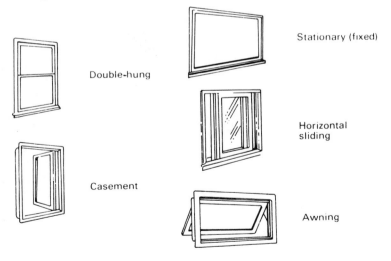

Double-hung

Stationary (fixed)

Horizontal sliding

Casement

Awning

Window types. Discounts can be had on all of these as well.

Most of these other window types are available in the same materials as double-hung, and the same buying and quality tips are relevant. It should be pointed out, however, that saving money on fixed windows will also depend on what you can settle for in terms of shape. As one contractor once told me, "The more curves, the more a fixed window will cost." Reason: it takes more work to manufacture it.

Also, a jalousie window, which is basically composed of movable glass slats, is poor for insulation purposes since much heat or cool air can escape even when the slats are closed.

BAY AND BOW WINDOWS

Bay and bow windows often are confused, but the one way I found to remember the difference is that a bow window is shaped like an arrow bow and a bay window isn't. It consists of a straight front that runs parallel to the house and has two angled sides.

When buying bay or bow windows, use the same tips as given for double-hung windows. Remember that if you add one of these windows it is like adding part of a room to your home, and that roof shingles and all the other materials you'd use in adding a room will have to be added.

Double-hung, 2' x 4" by 2' x 10": wood, $130; vinyl-clad wood, $185; aluminum, $195; vinyl, $172; aluminum-clad wood, $260.

CATALOG SHOPPING

There are at least three catalogs from which you can order and get some excellent buys, particularly on tools. Aside from the excellent buys, they can give an armchair view of what the prices are out there, so you can readily compare those to what stores are offering. In many cases I'm sure you'll decide to order from the catalog.

Following is a capsule description of each. All have 800 numbers.

Trendlines. These folks mainly sell brand-name hand and power tools. I think that in 99 percent of the cases their prices on tools will beat everyone else's.

The other one percent of the time try *Tool Crib*, a division of Acme Electric. They carry all kinds of power tools, ladders, bits, and some hand tools.

Tools on Sale is another good catalog source. They carry all kinds of tools, bits and the like. Prices are quite good. They are in St. Paul, Minnesota, and have an 800 number for anyone outside the state, and a 612 area code number within Minnesota.

Harbor Freight Tools. They, too, have excellent prices on brand-name hand and power tools. They also have their own line, Pittsburgh, which is comparable to Fuller and has very low prices indeed. Everything I've ever ordered in the Pittsburgh line has been good.

If the order is over $50, they don't charge for shipping.

Woodworker's Supply of Wyoming. This company sells all kinds of tools and doodads and items related to woodworking, such as nails. They deliver good prices and quality.

Note that if you order interstate you may not have to pay state tax. Also, when you call, ask if the tool is in stock. If it isn't, you may not want to endure the wait.

5

SAVING ON ELECTRICAL PRODUCTS AND MATERIALS

 I first learned about carded versus noncarded items when shopping one day for a switch. The loose switch was about half the price of the carded switch.

The only thing you lose—and it can be significant when electrical products are involved—is instruction on using the product.

Here, I would suggest you ask the dealer how to use the device, look at carded instructions, and/or visit your library. Though electricity is a scary subject to many people, doing-it-yourself is quite simple.

In addition to regular outlets such as hardware stores, home centers, and building supply yards, also look at prices offered by electrical supply stores. These cater to electricians, but they'll be happy to take your money—and give discounts—just as plumbing supply stores do.

One word about the UL or United Laboratories symbol on a product: I wouldn't buy a product that didn't have this symbol on it. UL is an independent agency and they test products for safety and then either "list" them or not. They won't say something's safe, just that it has passed tests and is listed. That's enough for me.

Following is a look at where you can save on a wide variety of electrical products and materials.

Boxes

Electrical boxes house switches and receptacles; they are made of metal and plastic, and in most cases plastic is much cheaper.

The caveat is that they must usually be used on new work only. They come with nails called "captive nails" mounted on them for attachment for open framing. Metal boxes, on the other hand, are available for new as well as "old" work, as they say in the trade. There is one standard plastic box which can be used like a metal "Gem" box. (The origin of the word "Gem" is not known.)

Normally, as mentioned, plastic is much cheaper than metal, but do check it out. I've seen plastic at higher prices.

Another way to save on plastic is on sales. Three or four times a year, and usually just before the autumn and spring, they are drastically reduced. I have bought boxes that normally sell for $.79 to $1.25 for a quarter each. In other words, four or five boxes for the price of one. At that rate I always make it a point to pick up a few.

Make sure you watch the fliers that home centers and hardware stores put out so you can spot the sales.

Plastic box, left, can cost a lot less than metal, right, but not always. Compare carefully.

Cable

The standard cable used for house wiring these days is Romex, either 14-2 (meaning 14 gauge, 2 wire) or 12-2 with ground. This cable is flattish, cream colored, easy to work with. In the old days BX was used, but now its use is restricted to special situations in many areas (such as wiring to an oil burner where its metal jacket can stand up better than Romex). BX is so much more difficult to work with that it's not regularly used unless the local electrical code requires it.

Romex comes in coils of 25, 50, 100 and 250 feet; the longer the coil, the less you'll pay. For example you might pay 12 cents a foot for 50 feet but 6 cents per foot for 250 feet.

BX, left, and Romex cable. Romex is sold by the foot and in various size boxes. The more you buy, the more you save.

Buying it in bulk coils is usually the best way to purchase it, unless you have a need for a short, specific length. Then it pays to just buy that much. Why buy a big coil and have a lot left over? On the other hand, you may have a bit left over on a large coil and still make out better than if you were to buy a specific length.

BX also comes in 250-foot coils and you can also buy it by the foot.

Circuit Breakers

Occasionally circuit breakers are on sale, but usually only at home centers and not at local hardware stores or electrical supply houses. Therefore, if you need installation advice you'll have to shop at a home center where the likelihood of getting solid advice is minimal, unless you shop at home centers that stress service (such as the Home Depot). If you know what you're doing, though, you can make out. Not too long ago, for example, I saw a Four D single breaker for sale for $8.99 at a local hardware store and the same breaker was selling for $11.99 at a local electrical supply store. If anything is to be saved, it's by shopping around.

Conduit

EMT, or electro-mechanical tubing, comes in 10' lengths and is the most commonly used metal pipe to run wire through inside or outside a house.

Savings aren't usually that significant unless you need a lot of EMT. It comes 10 pieces to the bundle and when you buy a bundle you can expect to save around 10 percent. Of course you can also save by comparison shopping.

EMT can only be used inside the house. If you have turns to make, fittings are used, or the pipe can be bent with a tool called a hickey, which you can rent or buy (though it doesn't seem to make sense as a purchase). Another electrical pipe is plastic. This comes, like EMT, in 10-foot lengths and various diameters. Plastic can be used inside as well as outside, but if turns are to be made, fittings must be used. For straight runs inside the house plastic would likely be much cheaper than EMT. The other type of conduit is heavy walled pipe. This comes in heavy gauges and can be used inside and outside the house. Its walls are heavier than EMT and it is used in many outside applications. It is the most expensive of the three materials.

Cord Sets

Cord sets consist of wire in certain lengths—depending on use—with terminals, plugs or bare wire leads ready to be attached. For example, a spotted black cord with a male plug on one end and a female plug on the other for use with griddles and the like is a cord set. You don't have to go through the trouble of preparing them (stripping the wire, etc.), for attachment. Cord sets are available for use with both small and large appliances.

Usually, you'll just buy these when needed and retailers know this, so they rarely put them on sale, though I have sometimes seen them on sale at home centers as a loss leader. You'll have to hope that your time of need dovetails with the saletime: it doesn't make a lot of sense to buy, say, a toaster wire and put it in reserve.

Extension cords are also considered cord sets and these most definitely are a sale item, simply because retailers know that people need them all the time; demand is high. They are frequently on sale, so it's just a matter of watching what's there.

As with other products, it's a good idea to know what you are buying so you get the proper quality. In this regard, orange-covered cords are good while flat yellow ones are usually lower quality. In other words, if you buy a yellow cord with the same electrical capacity you will usually not be getting the same quality though there are a few brands of yellow cords of good quality. However, brown and white cords are the same quality. Extension cords with a blue covering are top quality and are mainly used in marine applications. You can also get extension cords covered with green rubber, in case you want a cord that's going to be unobtrusive when running through grass, such as when you have the cord permanently in place providing power to a remote location. Otherwise, to use a green extension cord for everyday use is an unsafe practice: you want a colored cord so that you can see it.

When buying an extension cord, make sure you are comparing the same thing. The color of the cord alone is not enough. Cords come in different capacities, with two wires and no ground as well as a ground, and with various letters, such as SJ and SO indicating what kind of material, such as oil, the cord can stand up to. In other words, you want to be sure that you are comparing oranges to oranges.

Two extension cords, both ostensibly the same. But the flat yellow one, right, is not the quality of its orange counterpart, and my advice is to stay with the orange one.

Incidentally, extension cords come with ends which may be sockets, or bare wires which you can get to serve just about any purpose you need.

Also, you don't want to overbuy.

Finally, you can make your own extension cords by buying a length of wire of appropriate amperage and attaching plugs to it, though whether it's worth the effort is questionable.

Fuses

Standard fuses, known for some unfathomable reason as plug-in fuses even though they screw in place, are available in packages of four, and if you have a need for four in the same capacity (say 15 amps, which are used for lighting circuits in the house), that's fine. But if you only need one, probably the best place to buy them is your local hardware store. Reason: if you ask for just one fuse, the dealer will likely break open a package to sell you just the one, at one quarter the price of the package. Or, buy two and have one in reserve. You'll still save.

Cartridge fuses, the kind that look like shotgun shells, are sold loose. Just get what you need. They can be purchased 10 to the box for less cost, but it's highly unlikely that this would represent a bargain.

Lamp Parts

Many hardware stores carry a wide variety of lamp parts loose. Indeed, I went into one store in New Hampshire that had a big bin filled with maybe 30 tiny drawers, all filled with different lamp parts, everything from bushings to washers to replacement extension toggle switches to the connectors for bead chain. It's just a matter of asking for what you need. And this was just part of what was available.

For such an inventory of stuff you can also collect everything you need to build a lamp, and it is the way to go. Today manufacturers card lamp-building parts such as sockets and harps (the piece that protects the bulb) and rod in one package, but this is the expensive way to go. It's better to buy components loose.

Because the parts lineup is so complete, it can lead you to saving even more money. If a socket goes bad, for example, you don't have to buy the entire socket. Just buy the internal switch mechanism in it and replace it. You'll save yourself a buck or two.

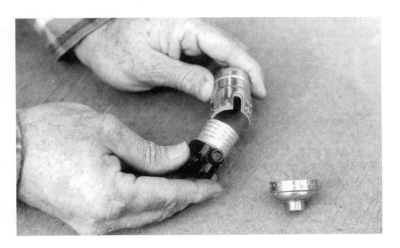

You can save on lamp sockets by only buying the interior mechanism, which, as you see, can be separated from the shell. It is typical. Everything can be broken down into tiny parts—and you can buy those parts at tiny parts rates.

Lampholders—the old-fashion porcelain lamps—also can be repaired by only replacing parts, not the whole lampholder. The parts are available.

Light Fixtures

Here, the best bet—and it's a heckuva good one—is to select the fixture you want and then ask for a discount. I've heard of 60 percent discounts in electrical supply stores.

You can also visit home centers. In recent years the variety and looks and quality of light fixtures at home centers has improved greatly, and the prices are right. This doesn't mean, as I said in Chapter One, that you can't get a discount. Just ask for it, or for the "on sale price." You may well get it, unless the retailer has cut his prices on fixtures to the bone, which is highly unlikely.

When shopping around for a fixture you can and should get particular brand and model numbers off the box.

Incidentally, all necessary parts for hanging a lamp can be bought either carded or loose.

Plugs

A variety of plugs is available. For cords, there are quick-clamp replacement types. The way to save here is to buy them loose instead of packaged. For example, I recently bought a couple of unpackaged quick-clamp plugs for 69 cents each. The same plug in a package cost $1.59—more than double the price.

There are also specialized plugs for appliances, standard light plugs and more. Many of these are available loose; all you have to do is find the outlet(s).

This is Nirvana: lots of loose electrical items, at better prices than carded stuff. (Site: Laurel Hardware, Northport, New York)

Receptacles

Here, again, you have loose versus packaged, so just get the loose.

Another way to save is to not overbuy. You can get 15 amp and 20 amp or spec (specification) outlets, but they will cost more. There are really only two instances in which you should use 20 amp: in the bathroom and kitchen, because these tend to get a lot of use and the 20 amp is typically a heavier, better-made product than the 15 amp.

Packaged switch at left costs three times what loose and boxed switch costs—and they're all the same.

You can also save if you buy bulk; you'll get 10 receptacles in a box. And you'll have better luck getting boxes of receptacles from electrical supply houses.

Switches

You can buy switches 10 to the box and save. You can also go the loose versus packaged route on standard as well as a wide variety of small switches, such as cord switches (the switch is installed in the line), canopy switches (control lamps), and much more.

Wall Plates

Plain plastic or metal wall plates are cheap, but the prices on fancy wood wall plates are unreal ($5 or $6 or much more).

I have shopped the heck out of these and have yet to find them at a human price, though looking around will yield some savings.

I don't buy them out of principle. If I want a fancier wall plate, I just cover it with wallcovering or Contact. For just pennies you can simulate anything from leather to fine wood.

Wire

Hardware stores and home centers sell all kinds of different wire from reels by the foot. Prices can vary quite a bit, so if you need a lot of it, it would definitely pay to shop around.

Wire Connectors

These are commonly called wire nuts, and they are actually used to join Romex or BX cable. The wire ends are stripped and the wire nuts are twisted on the ends, then taped.

These come in a variety of sizes and colors to accommodate various wire sizes, and they come loose and packaged. 'Nuff said.

6

SAVING ON PLUMBING PRODUCTS AND MATERIALS

As mentioned before, plumbing supply outlets, which once only would deal with plumbers, now are more than happy to do business with the ordinary customer.

Also, big discounts are possible (markups on fixtures are around 50 percent). Plumbing supply outlets tend to charge the list price to the retail customer, but once you know this is only a starting point, you'll be fine.

Interestingly, the big three in plumbing—Kohler, American Standard and Eljer—now supply products to home centers, something that was verboten in the past. This means that you can be assured of quality products when you buy at home centers. Brand name is instructive, and these companies have not been around for as long as they have because they make poor products.

Aerators

These come in a number of different sizes and qualities including models with triple stainless steel screens. Cost is in the $4–$5 range, but there are also plastic models that work well and will cost you $2 or $3 less.

Bath Accessories

Bath accessories are right up there with kitchen cabinets and fancy wall plates in terms of being obscenely overpriced. I would strongly suggest that you bargain for a 30 percent to 40 percent reduction on these things. Indeed, if you are buying them as part of a bath package of fixtures you'll have that much more leverage.

It is not possible to give any tips on brand names because there are so many that one would end up comparing apples to pears.

My advice here is to look over as many accessories as you can. Carefully examine the finish. Is it marred, pitted, not consistent? And what is the accessory made of? If it's not stated, ask the retailer what it is. After a while you will get a sense of what you're buying and its quality.

Also, check the warranty. As stated in Appendix B, what the manufacturer does or doesn't guarantee can tell you a lot.

Faucets, Standard

Two-handled faucets for sinks, lavatories and tubs are made of a number of materials: pot metal, tubular brass, plastic, and cast brass.

Pot metal can look good with a chrome finish, but it isn't. It readily rots out. Tubular brass is better, but the gauge is not all that heavy. Plastic faucets were characterized by one plumber I know as worse than useless.

The only material really worth considering—at least for the long run—is cast brass. Cast brass faucets have heavy-gauge brass bodies and quality mechanical innards: companies who put quality into the body also put it into the working parts. (A cast brass faucet is heavy: heft it and any other type and you'll immediately feel the difference.)

Cast brass faucet, left, is heavy. Lift it and the pot metal version, right, and you'll feel the difference.

Faucets are either the compression or washerless type. In the first case, as you turn the handle a threaded fluted metal shaft, known as the stem or spindle, turns up or down in the faucet body, which is correspondingly threaded. On the bottom of the stem is a rubber or plastic washer. When you turn the handle all the way off, this washer processes against the hole where the water emerges (called the seat), plugging it up. Turn the handle on and the stem lifts off and the water flows out.

The washerless type involves a ball or cartridge sliding over the opening. When holes in the ball or cartridge align in the faucet body, the water is allowed to flow; when not in alignment, the water is blocked off.

Exploded view of a single-handle washerless faucet.

Peerless washerless faucet. Faucets don't have to be pedestrian in looks.

This is actually a spray hose, which works like a faucet.

Faucet prices, of course, vary greatly. For a standard item that will serve well and looks good, expect to pay anywhere from $30 to $70 for a lavatory faucet, depending on style and whether the faucet comes with a pop-up drain mechanism; $60 to $110 for the kitchen faucet depending on style and finish (brass-plated, nickel-plated, chrome-plated, etc.) and whether it comes with or without a spray hose; $60 to $150 for a tub faucet depending on style and elaborateness.

Your best bet is to buy by brand names. I think the following are good: Kohler, Eljer, American Standard, Delta, and Peerless. The Peerless line is particularly geared to the do-it-yourselfer.

Another good faucet, which has come on like gangbusters recently with its advertising campaign is Price Pfister. They make good, reasonably priced faucets.

I would definitely stay away from off brands.

Another brand is Moen. I like all their metal faucets.

One way to determine quality on any faucet is to check the warranty and see what it guarantees and what it doesn't, and for how long. Does it guarantee mechanical innards as well as finish? It should.

Faucets, Temperature Control

A few days ago I saw a movie in which a man and woman were arguing, the man in the shower, the woman at the sink. The argument reached a boiling point, one might say, and the woman flushed the toilet, making the man yelp with pain.

The temperature control faucet is supposed to control this type of problem. If the water temperature suddenly changes, a diaphragm in the faucet goes instantaneously into action to stabilize the water temperature.

If you buy one, I believe Symmons is probably the best one around.

Faucet prices can vary greatly from outlet to outlet. You may be able to find one you like that is available in a number of outlets. If not you can always, as suggested, go to a plumbing supply store or a hardware store and ask for a discount. I would suggest again that you know in advance which model you're interested in.

Faucet Parts

For compression and washerless faucets a variety of repair parts are available. Following is a lineup.

WASHERS

Washers periodically go bad. To save money for the moment, you can buy a single washer in the size needed for 10 cents or so. But take the bad washer to the store to ensure getting the correct size; washers that are the same nominal or named size can differ among brand names. For example, a so-called "quarter" washer made by three different companies can be three different actual sizes.

For convenience, you can pick up a boxed assortment of washers. These contain seven or eight washers in different sizes and a few brass screws. You are likely to be able to minister to every faucet in the house with just this one box. Indeed, chances are you'll never use all the washers, which is a waste, but we are not talking megabucks here (more like $1.50 per box) and you will have them on hand should the faucet start to drip when you're trying to get some sleep. (Tip: make sure the package says the screws are brass. Some chintzy manufacturers actually save pennies by providing steel screws, which simply can't stand up to water.)

Washers come flat and beveled (in profile they're slanted on top); for replacement use the beveled type—they seal better. Washers are also made, as mentioned above, of neoprene and rubber. The price is the same but you'll save if you buy neoprene because they last longer.

STEMS

These are the spindles, or threaded handle shafts also mentioned earlier—the part that the handle is attached to at the top.

For some reason, stems are available in *hundreds,* maybe *thousands,* of different sizes. (It's probably because each faucet manufacturer wanted to make sure only his replacement stems could be bought for his particular brand of faucet.)

Sometimes, therefore, it is difficulty to get a replacement (which is another good reason for buying a brand name faucet: replacement parts are more readily available).

Think about using a no-rotate washer, which can be bought for a quarter or so and installed on any stem and make it like new. The device consists of a metal rim which houses a washer and friction prongs. The prongs are forced into the end of the stem, locking the no-rotate washer in place. In effect, you create a new stem which costs much less (a total of 90 cents) than the $10 or $12 you'd pay should you find a replacement stem. (Just recently Dave Shannon paid *$28* for a stem.)

When buying the stem itself, though, use the phone to see if the stem for your particular faucet is in stock and how much it costs. Well-stocked hardware stores are your best bet. Visit a few places for prices. Some

Faucet stem. Sizes vary greatly—and cost $10 and much more.

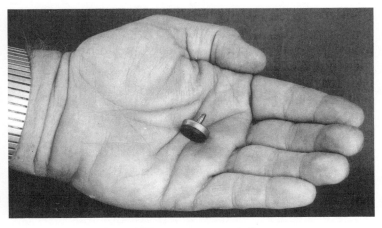

No-rotate washer. When a stem fails, you can renew it with this 90-cent part, a terrific saving.

hardware store dealers are greedy, and like to stick it to the consumer on such an esoteric item as a stem.

SEATS

The seat is the hole in the faucet body against which the end of the spindle presses to block and allow water flow. Washers wear out first, but eventually the seat gets pitted and no matter how hard you turn the faucet off, it leaks.

In some faucets, the seat is not replaceable—it's just a hole in the metal—but in many cases it is. It consists of a circle of metal with a threaded portion and screws into the faucet body. If you peer down into the faucet body with a flashlight and see a square or hex-sided hole, you'll know it's replaceable. It is removed with a faucet seat wrench, which is an L-shaped tool with ends machined to match the shape of the seat.

I don't know any way to save money on these (except the money saved by trying a few hardware stores to compare prices), but I wanted to make you aware of it so that you don't inadvertently discard the faucet when you can in fact renew it. Seats are cheap anyway, costing around 75 cents each.

HANDLES

If a faucet handle goes bad, there's no need to buy an entire new faucet. Many different styles of handles are available. You'll pay top price for a direct replacement handle from the manufacturer; $12 is not an unusual price.

There are also handles which are not made by the original manufacturer and these cost a lot less—say $6.

And, if you can't find a handle that fits, you can get a universal fit handle for $4 or so. Here, you slip the handle over the stem and then tighten a set screw (it's permanently attached to the handle) to secure it. There are enough styles available so you won't miss getting the same thing as the original and you can save quite a bit.

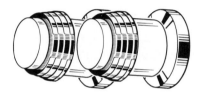

Universal replacement handles from Fluidmaster. Such handles cost a fraction of what direct replacement handles would cost.

WASHERLESS FAUCET PARTS

Replacement parts are available for both the ball and cartridge type faucets, but it's better economy—the faucets will last longer—if you replace the cartridge in the cartridge faucet and get a kit that contains all necessary parts for rejuvenating the ball type. The problem is that if one part goes bad, you have to wonder how far behind the other parts are.

If you have trouble finding any part (for anything) at home centers or hardware stores, by all means go to a plumbing supply store. They stock thousands of parts loose, and the quality is generally high.

Fittings

Fittings are the vari-shaped pieces that are used with water and waste pipe and do three different things: extend pipe, enable it to change direction, and allow you to change from one pipe material, say galvanized, to another. Like pipe (below), fittings are made of a variety of materials: plastic, galvanized metal, copper, brass, and cast iron.

FITTINGS FOR WATER PIPE

Copper is the most common pipe used in America and three kinds of fittings are used to join it: sweat, compression, and flare. Sweat fittings are called that because they are soldered to the pipe by heat, and when heated, the beads of solder drip like sweat. Of all the fittings, they are by far the most commonly used.

Compression fittings are used to join pipe without heat. They are threaded. Sleeves and nuts are slipped over the ends of the pipe, the pipe ends are placed inside the fitting, and then the nuts are slid down to the ends of the fittings and screwed on tightly.

Flare fittings are similarly installed, but a flaring tool is used to expand or flare the ends of the pipe before the fittings are drawn tight against them.

Flare fittings are common where using a flame would be hazardous, like compression fittings but, more important, where you need as perfect a seal as possible, such as when installing oil or gas lines.

The way to save money on copper waterpipe fittings is to use sweat fittings whenever possible. For example, a ½″ copper elbow sweat fitting costs about 19 cents. The same size compression fittings would set you back about $2.29, and a comparable flare fitting would cost $3.40.

Sweat soldering may seem like a big deal, but it's not. It's simple to learn and it is certainly worth it. The library is loaded with plumbing books, and highly detailed information is available on the process. (Reference 643.7 has a lot of plumbing books.)

Sweat fittings come loose and carded. As usual, you can save—around 10 percent—by buying loose. That can add up if you need a lot of fittings.

Also, shop around. Since sweat fittings are so common there is competition and, consequently, prices are lower. You'll probably do best at home centers.

Flare fittings are made even more expensive by the necessity of having to use the flaring tool, which could set you back about $30. The way to save here is to rent the tool. A local rental agency quoted a price of $5.00 for the day.

FITTINGS FOR WASTE

In the old days, cast iron waste pipe was put together carefully and skillfully by plumbers only using hot lead and a packing material called oakum.

Today, "No Hub" or hubless cast iron, which is considerably thinner and has straight rather than bell-shaped (expanded) ends, is mostly used: the ends of the pipe are slipped into a recess around the neoprene fitting and then stainless steel wormgear clamps are tightened to a certain "torque" to seal the fitting.

Shop around for these fittings. The best possible source is home centers.

A variation on the hubless fittings are Fernco (the most common brand name), which are simply formed rubber sections which slip over the ends of the pipe and then are secured with clamps. Fernco fittings are expensive ($3–$15) and, again, shopping around is the best way to go.

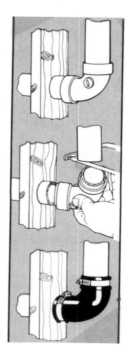

Fernco fitting in action. It allows repair—and no pipe replacement.

Plastic waste pipe fittings are another item that it is well worth shopping around for.

Lavatories

In the language of the trade, bathroom sinks are called lavatories, or lavs. (There's a Latin word *lavare*, which means to wash. And of course there's the soap, Lava.)

The first way to save on lavatories is, of course, to know what you're buying. Lavatories come in five basic materials.

Enameled steel is steel with a porcelain coating. It is light—and cheap—but its big bugaboo is that if something is dropped on it, it will chip.

Vitreous china lavatory is constructed of the same material used to make toilets. It makes an excellent lavatory.

Enameled cast iron is widely regarded as the best material for a lavatory. Cast iron is a strong, durable, heavy metal. Like the enameled steel, the cast iron has a coating of enamel, but unlike steelcast iron it doesn't flex and therefore doesn't chip as readily. The enamel coating is also thicker.

Cast polymer refers to a variety of materials whose base is a polyester resin which is mixed with marble chips, aluminum, granite or glass. The resulting form is coated with a protective gel coat. Cast polymer is availble in solid colors but also imitates other materials. The most common type is "cultured marble," which resembles the real thing.

All the above lavatories are designed to stand alone; the vanity is separate.

Solid surface materials are lavatory and vanity in one. Corian, Nevamar, Avenite or the like is used for this.

Unlike cast polyester, which only has a surface coating, the design and color of solid surface material go all the way through.

To be able to compare and contrast lavs properly, and to ensure some certainty of quality, I would suggest, if you like cast iron, enameled steel, or vitreous china, that you stick to top companies: Kohler, Eljer, and American Standard. They make many different models, colors, and styles and the prices differ significantly by hundreds of dollars. The good news, however, is that you can get an inexpensive lavatory that still has good quality. For example, you can get a cast iron lavatory for $200 or $900 and the quality will be the same: what you pay for is the shape, style, and color of the bowl.

Your first step is to decide what you want. You can browse through kitchen/bath showrooms, or home centers, or even through plumbing supply houses, which often have vignettes, as they say in the trade, and you can see the sample lavatories. If you like one, note its price and model number and then start shopping around in earnest. Ask how much the lav is at the outlet where you've seen it, then check the other outlets for price. Most important, ask how much the dealer will take off the price he gives you.

Another way to do it is to check out home centers to see what lavs they have on sale.

When making comparisons, make sure you have the right model. The best bet is to get the model number. You can also save an additional 15 percent to 20 percent by buying a white lav instead of a colored one: color costs.

Savings on Corian and other solid surface materials can also be achieved by shopping around, and you can also save by checking out cultured marble. This comes with gel coats that vary from 16 to 20 mills, so when comparing prices make sure you are comparing products with the same gel coat thickness. To ensure quality, it is important to make sure that the lavatory carries the seal of the Cultured Marble Institute.

Lavatory Parts

Any lavatory installation is made up of a number of drain pipes, water supply tubes, and a drain mechanism.

The trap—so called because it traps water as a seal against gases and vermin getting into the house—is actually composed of a number of different parts, as follows.

The J bend is a piece of pipe shaped like the letter. It extends down from the tailpiece section of the lavatory, which is itself a short, straight piece of pipe.

The J bend is available in "rough brass" (uncoated). This is good if the lav pipes don't show. It costs around $3.98. For a couple of dollars more you can buy chrome-covered brass. This is normally used when the pipes show.

Cheapest of all is the plastic J bend, but unfortunately it tends to come loose and leaks occur. My advice is to avoid it.

The wall bend is the piece of pipe that is connected to the J bend and goes into the wall. The same things that can be said about the J bend apply to it (except it's a little more expensive).

The waste bend is the old-fashioned pipe that, with the J bend, forms an S-shaped trap, commonly called an S trap. It is often used with a pedestal-type sink because it can be hidden inside the pedestal. All of these parts come carded and loose and in boxes; you'll save a bit more buying boxed.

Trap. Note J bend portion defined by nuts.

Pop-up mechanism.
You save $20 if you buy it with faucet.

The drain assembly is called the pop-up plug assembly. If you have a choice, definitely buy it along with the faucet, as part of the purchase. Bought this way it's cheap, maybe $5 above the price of the faucet. For example, the faucet might cost you $45; with the pop-up mechanism it's $50. On the other hand, if you buy it separately it will set you back $20 or so.

Pipe

Once again the key is to shop around. Good buys are possible on hubless cast iron, copper water pipe, and plastic waste pipe. Home centers and plumbing supply stores sell it in long lengths, but if you need it shorter you can get it in hardware stores. They sell in 10', 5' and 3' lengths.

Whether or not you can—or should—use plastic water pipe is debatable. Many plumbers say that CPVC, or chlorinated polyvinyl chloride, which is used for hot water, "spaghettis" or bends and sags under the high heat generated by hot water.

Problems have been reported with cold water plastic, or PVC. The high pressure that is generated within the pipes blows the fittings, which are glued on.

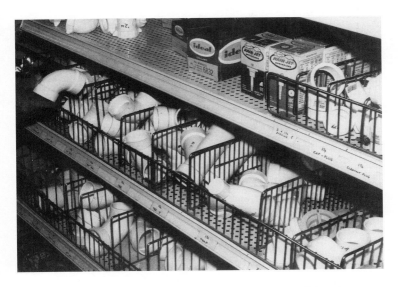

Plastic waste pieces. Plastic works well and is cheap.

On the other hand, plastic waste pipe, which is not subject to pressure or high heat, gets high marks from plumbers. Additionally, the savings are great, a minimum of at least 50 percent less than other types.

If you wish, you can use plastic waste pipe with other types of pipe and save. For example, if you wanted to replace a section of copper waste pipe you could do it with plastic, using adapters to connect it to the existing copper pipe. You'd have to calculate whether or not the price of the plastic pipe section plus adapters would be less than simply replacing the section with copper, or whatever the pipe happens to be.

Sinks

Like lavatories, sinks are available in a variety of types. Cast iron is the Cadillac of sinks, a heavy rigid metal coated with enamel (porcelain) that is quite durable.

Porcelain on steel is the least expensive sink you can buy, but it is also the least durable of all sinks. It will wear out and chip more quickly than cast iron and stainless.

Stainless steel sinks are the most popular for the kitchen, but here one has to be very careful because the metal comes in various gauges, or thicknesses. The heaviest gauge is 20 but you can also get it as thin as 16. The best stainless costs more than cast iron. Finishes vary, from highly polished to a dull, brushed look.

As with lavatories, the best bet is to stay within big brand names: Eljer, American Standard, and Kohler.

I think you should consider only one brand of stainless: Elkay. They make sinks of varying quality, but they're all good. The "Celebrity" is their best.

Toilets

Toilets come in one-piece and two-piece styles. The one-piece is just that: bowl and water tank are one formed piece. They are known also as siphon jet toilets, which refers to the way they flush (very quietly). They are also sleek and very well designed.

One-piece siphon jet toilet (Kohler).

Two-piece toilet. The tank rests on the back of the bowl. Two-piece is cheaper than one-piece.

The two-piece toilet refers to a toilet with a separate tank and bowl: the water tank sits on the back of the bowl and can be disconnected if necessary.

One-piece toilets cost considerably more than two-piece, so if you want to save money your first step would be to opt for the two-piece kind.

Another way to save is on color. As with other fixtures, you can save 15 percent to 20 percent if you buy a white toilet. Color costs, and so manufacturers have two kinds of color, regular and super which costs even more. (I assume that it costs them more to manufacture a toilet with these super colors.)

When you buy a toilet, you may or may not get a seat with it, so note this carefully when shopping. It can make a difference of $25 or more in price. Even if a toilet comes with a seat, you can buy your own separately.

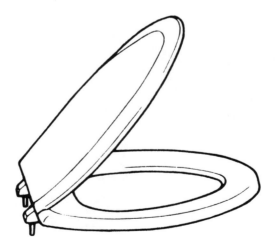

Toilet seat. Pay attention to whether the seat comes with the toilet. The seat can add $25 or more to the price.

As with lavatories, a key in buying a toilet is to buy brand names; specifically Kohler, American Standard, and Eljer. It should be noted, though, that even though you pay hundreds of dollars of differences you will not get a better toilet, but merely one with better style. For example, American Standard's one-piece Lexington is no better than the Cadet, which costs hundreds less. Toilets are made of vitreous china and this simply will not vary from bowl to bowl: vitreous china is vitreous china.

The working parts of the toilet don't vary much, either. The big three make quality mechanical innards, period.

Of course as with lavatories, it can pay handsomely to shop around. Start at the home center and see what they have on sale. If you like it, contact your local plumbing supply outlet to see what price they can give. And don't forget to ask for a discount of 15 percent or 20 percent. That might make the plumbing supply outlet lower than the home center.

If you don't see anything you like, then pore over manufacturer's brochures, or magazines, until you spot something, and then do a price inquiry.

Toilet Parts

All parts of a toilet are replaceable. Following is a lineup.

The ballcock is the water controlling device. It lets in new water when the tank empties to flush the bowl. Ballcocks rival stems in terms of different models available, and if part of the ballcock goes bad you can begin a search that may end up with you using another part of the bath. You'll need a cold shower so you can regain your sanity.

A better way is to buy a complete replacement ballcock.

These are sized to fit almost all toilets (though there are exceptions). An even better solution, in my view, is to replace the ballcock with a diaphragm type ballcock, such as Fluidmaster makes. They sell two versions, one with an anti-siphon feature: it prevents waste water from being siphoned or routed into the water supply system. They are easy to install and a lot cheaper than a regular ballcock, costing around $5 versus around $10.

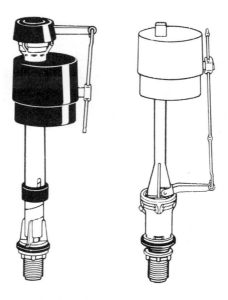

Two Fluidmaster ballcock mechanisms. They are much cheaper than standard ballcocks.

The tank ball is the ball that lowers when the water level in the tank goes down. Eventually they open up, get some water in them, and lose buoyancy, and replacement is called for.

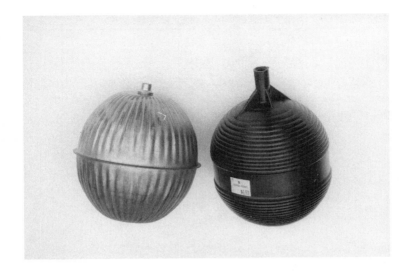

The copper tank ball costs $4.50 while the black plastic costs $1.67—and it is better.

Tank balls come in copper and plastic. Copper costs three times as much as plastic and doesn't last as long, so get the plastic.

The flush valve seat is the donut-shaped section with a threaded part that passes through the bottom of the tank on a two-piece toilet and to which the big toilet waste pipe is linked.

When this goes bad—it becomes pitted—it can be difficult to replace, and sometimes it means that the entire toilet must be changed.

To avoid this, I suggest you get yourself a Flusher Fixit kit to renew the seat without having to take the toilet apart. Instructions come with the unit, but basically it just involves gluing a seat on the existing seat to create a smooth surface.

Flusher fixer. It lets you fix the valve in the toilet tank, possibly saving the toilet itself. The device only costs $3 or $4.

The cost of the Flusher Fixer is about $5 and that sure beats the cost of a new toilet.

The overflow is the large-diameter vertical tube that sits in the tank and into which excess water in the tank will spill over and run down into the toilet.

Refill tubes made of plastic or brass are threaded at the bottom. Plastic works *well on new work but not existing tanks.*

A variety of water supply tubes are available including chrome-covered copper, stainless flexible, and plastic. Price varies from about $7 or $8 for the flexible type to a dollar or so for the plastic. The plastic is flexible and cheap, and you can use it quite successfully and save.

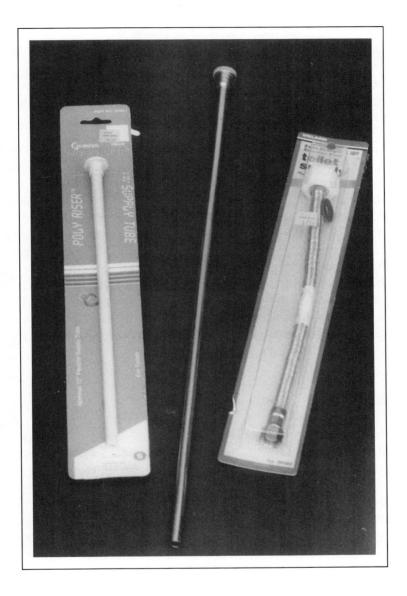

Toilet supply tubes. Plastic, left, costs a buck and change and works fine. Copper, middle, costs about $2. The flexible supply on right costs $7 and change.

Various other items are available including hinge bolts, bolt caps—you name it. Again, if you can't find a part in home centers try the plumbing supply store—and ask for it. Don't assume it doesn't exist. It does.

Tubs

You can get tubs made of enameled steel, plastic or fiberglass, or enameled cast iron. Cast iron is the first choice. A cast-iron tub is the best kind you can buy, and I recommend you get one but stay within brand name lines. You'll only pay about an average of $100 more than you would for enameled steel, but cast iron won't pit, be noisy, or chip. As with other fixtures, shop around at home centers, plumbing supply outlets and even kitchen and bath centers and showrooms, and don't forget to ask for discounts.

Tub Parts

Here, again, a variety of parts are available, including drain pieces, shower heads, and more. These items come carded but also loose. Get the loose, need I say.

You can also get a complete new plastic drain mechanism for around $11, as opposed to brass for $20, and it will work quite well. One good brand name is Peerless.

If the mechanism has gone on the blink and you want to avoid the expense of a new drain mechanism, just use an ordinary plug. It's cheap and it still works.

Shower arms are also replaceable.

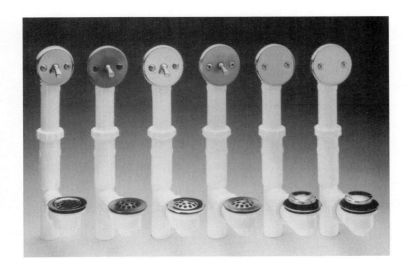

Plastic (and brass) drain mechanism from Peerless. They cost an average of $11 and work fine. Brass would cost about $20.

Shower arm. Again, all parts are replaceable on just about everything.

7

SAVING ON MISCELLANEOUS PRODUCTS AND MATERIALS

Adhesives

Carpenter's glue. This thick yellow glue is THE glue for woodworking. It comes in various sizes and if you intend to use a lot of it the gallon size is much less costly than the smaller squeeze bottles. For example, a gallon jug of yellow glue costs around $15, while in 8-ounce squeeze bottles it would cost about $3.00—or almost *$50 a gallon.*

If it is kept tightly closed, yellow glue stays fresh indefinitely. A handy applicator can be made by drilling a hole in the lid of a baby food jar and inserting a flux brush into it. The glue can be swabbed on easily, and it will also stay fresh in the jar.

Contact cement is mainly used for adhering plastic laminate to a countertop. As the name suggests, it

Carpenter's glue. A quart, left, cost $7.29; 8 ounces, one quarter as much, cost $3.19, and 4 ounces cost half of that, $2.19. Bigger is better.

adheres materials on contact. It comes in various forms, but the least expensive kind, the standard, works well in most situations. Whatever the type (latex, another type, is expensive and not recommended), the way to save when applying it to large sheets of materials is to do it with a stippled roller. This is a roller with a pebbled surface and when rolled out only the high spots on the roller apply glue; the spaces between don't, and that's glue saved, though the bonding job will be perfectly adequate. But to make this worthwhile you'd have to do a lot of gluing. The roller costs around $3.

Adhesive for wallcoverings comes in three different ways: wheat, which is a powder you mix with water;

The best bet is to buy big and then make a glue storage unit from baby food jar. Make a hole in the lid and keep the bristles of a small flux brush submerged in glue when not in use.

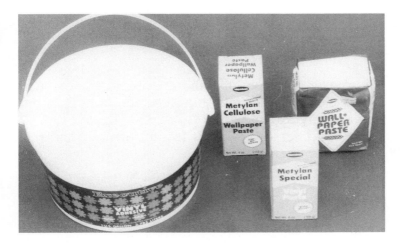

Wallpaper paste. The prepared paste, left, is five times the cost of others. Wheat paste is very cheap.

cellulose, for vinyl; and heavy cellulose. Wheat is really just for paper but the others may be interchangeable. Since they come prepared and ready-to-mix, do it yourself and save a lot over the prepared version.

Caulking

The Cadillac of caulks is silicone—it also is the most expensive caulk ($5 a cartridge versus $2.50 for the most acrylic latex and for oil-base). If you want to use silicone but don't like its price, do this: Use the inexpensive oil base as a base for the silicone, using the latter only to fill the top half inch. This way you'll have the weather resistance of silicone without the price.

Caulks often come with rebates. Heed the warnings in the box in Chapter One: You want to make sure that the date is okay and the package has the section on it that you are to send to the manufacturer.

Cements

For smaller patching jobs, the premixed cement, such as those sold by Sakrete and Acecrete, work fine, but they are very expensive.

Far better for a big job is to rent a mixer and mix cement from scratch.

Driveway Sealers

For sealing driveways, three basic kinds of black seal coatings are made: asphalt-based, latex-based and coal tar—based.

The asphalt-based material is difficult to apply, dries very slowly, and remains tacky for a long time. It is not recommended.

The latex base is easy to apply but it also gets a thumbs down because it doesn't hold up and comes off the surface.

The coal tar–base type is recommended, but you have to make sure you buy quality. I have always used Velvetop with good results.

The way to save on driveway sealer is to apply it correctly, minimizing its use. Most people apply it too thickly. In fact, it's better to apply one thin coat each year than one thick coat every few years.

First, the driveway should be wet with a hose and allowed to dry for an hour or so. Then apply a thin coat of the sealer. Make sure it is completely mixed; use a stick. A device that is also good is a small can screwed to a stick, which can be used as both a stirrer and scooper. Remember to fill cracked areas a little extra heavily.

This method can yield dramatic savings. One person I know used to use five 5-gallon cans of sealer; now he uses only *1½*.

Incidentally, you can save your tools by cleaning them immediately after use with water.

Drop Cloths

For covering up for interior paint jobs, there are three degrees, you might say, or drop cloths: make your own (almost) or use fairly thick plastic or canvas.

When I was a professional house painter, I had a bunch of canvas drop cloths that I carried from job to job, but these days when interior painting is to be done I find that I can get by very well—and very cheaply—as follows: lay overlapped sheets of newspapers on the floor, cover them with the thinnest plastic drop cloths, and cover those with old sheets or other cloths. The newspaper is fine for protecting any kind of flooring material (big sheets of cardboard, such as from a refrigerator box, also work well) and plastic, while very light and subject to lifting from the slightest breeze, is nevertheless impermeable and the sheets do a good job of holding it down.

Last time I checked, the thin plastic 9' x 12' drop cloths were going for 25 cents or so. Just discard them after use.

Next up the line of drop cloths are the 9' x 12' plastic sheets of various thicknesses, or mils. For a drop cloth, I would suggest the 3 mil thickness. You can also get plastic 50 feet long by 10 feet wide and 100 feet in a 2-mil thickness (called Redi roll) a lot cheaper. It comes folded up so it's convenient to unroll it as needed. Figure around $4 for a 10' x 25' section.   Canvas drop cloths come in regular, heavy, and extra heavy. I'd suggest the extra heavy because it drapes better and paint spatters can't get through (this can happen, crazily enough, with lighter drop cloths).

Fans, Whole House

For cooling the house, a whole house fan, which mounts in a ceiling at a strategic point and sucks hot air out, is a good idea. Here, again, it's a question of sticking to a brand name. I would stay with Nutone, Hunter, Fasco, or Emerson.

Whole house fans commonly go on sale, and have

various capacities. Make sure when buying one that you are comparing apples to apples.

Glazing Compound

This is the material that is used to seal the space between the glass and the frame. You can save by buying larger sizes if you need that much.

Two brands that I like are UGL and DAP. They are easy to apply, which cannot be said of all glazing compounds.

Ladders

Stepladders and extension ladders are essential for the diyer around the home, and there are various types and prices.

Stepladders come 4', 5', and 6' high and are made of wood, fiberglass, and aluminum. They also have safety rating standards, based on their construction, of 3, 2, 1 and 1A, with 1A being the best.

I think a 6' aluminum ladder of Class 2 safety will do the job. Wood is ungainly and tends to break down, while fiberglass is expensive. When buying the ladder, make sure you are comparing the same classes.

Ladder prices vary greatly so it would be a good idea to keep your eyes open for the best prices.

It's the same story with extension ladders, which come anywhere from 16'—extended—up. If you have a relatively short house a 16-foot aluminum ladder will do fine. If your house is taller you should go that much higher. I would stay away from wood. If you are chary of electricity, get a fiberglass ladder—but be prepared to pay.

On an extension ladder, where life and limb are at risk, I would go for the Class 1 ladder. Cost varies, again. For a 16-foot aluminum ladder figure $190.

Lubricants

Light household oil, such as "3-in-1" brand, comes in 1-ounce and 3-ounce cans. The 3-ounce can is more economical but both are expensive.

You can use non-detergent motor oil for household tasks. Make sure it's non-detergent. Use a cheap oil can as a dispenser. The savings are large.

The way to save is to buy the quart size of *non-detergent* motor oil. You can't use motor oil with detergent in it: the detergent component will destroy any rubber seals, such as on a motor, that the oil is used on. You can use any 20-weight detergent labeled non-detergent. For ease of use, obtain an inexpensive plastic oil can for $1.60 or so and fill it as needed. The savings will be large, and you can use the oil on anything that you would use light household oil on, such as oil burner motors or garage doors.

Paints

Interior and exterior paint. As one hardware store owner in New Hampshire put it: "The best way to get a bargain on paint is to watch for sales. Paint is always on sale."

This is emphatically true, and it is not unusual to be able to save $5 to $10 a gallon. If you are painting, say, the outside of your house and need 10 gallons, that's $50 or $100 saved.

Of course to know that you're getting a bargain, you need to know standard prices. You can get a sense of these by glancing at paint ads from time to time, or by observing prices when you go into a home center or paint or hardware store.

Paint sales are many times held in the spring, but an even better time to shop is in January. Of course, unless you live in an area where the temperatures are right, you won't be able to paint the exterior, but this needn't prevent you from buying the paint and storing it until you are ready to use it. (Make sure latex paint is stored above 60 degrees Fahrenheit.)

You should plan the job so that you don't have to buy any quart sizes of paint. By the quart, the price of paint can easily double, so if you have to pick up an extra quart or two you waste money.

Paint is also available in 2- and 5-gallon *plastic* containers. Sometimes these cost much less than by the gallon, so check them out if you need a lot of paint in one color.

Some stores will charge you for mixing paint to the shade you want, while others won't.

Paint comes in a bewildering array of brands. Again, I think you should stick to the brand names here. For me, Benjamin Moore is the best, so when I get it I usually shop a local paint store that has good prices—they deal with painters all the time—and get the price plus a discount if I'm buying a substantial amount. This way I know I'm getting a quality paint, something that cannot be determined with store brands without intensive analysis of the ingredients. In general, good paint costs, so if you see something for $5 or $6 a gallon you can figure it's not very good. I hear that Pratt & Lambert, Sears, and Sherwin-Williams are good, so if you see these on sale it's probably a good idea to buy. Above all, to risk redundancy, you don't want to buy a particular paint simply because it's cheap. Bargain basement paint can be difficult to use, cover badly, and fade quickly. Paint quality is related to how much pigment is used in the manufacturing process, and some companies don't use much at all.

Make sure, by the way, that you buy a manufacturer's top-of-the-line material. Moore's best is Moorglo for interior and Moorgard for exteriors. Brand name isn't enough. Moore, for example, makes other grades, which I would not recommend as highly as their top brand.

You can also save by darkening paint. Sometimes a ceiling may be so dark that it would seem to need two coats of paint. Maybe so, but you can often save giving it two coats by beefing up the first coat—giving it more hiding power—by adding lamp black colorant to the can. Use half a tube of colorant per gallon. Cost is around $2 per tube. This will make it ever so slightly darker—it even may look a little gray in the can—but it will dry white and you will save the cost of another coat (typically a half gallon of paint) as well as the labor.

You can give color paint additional hiding power the same way. A wide variety of colorants are available in tubes and cans.

Incidentally, you should not use more than a tube per gallon. Otherwise, the colorant won't mix in properly and can show up as darker colored streaks when you apply the paint.

If you have a choice, esthetically or otherwise, use darker instead of lighter colors in your home to avoid having to do a costly two-coat job.

Paint Removers

This is a very expensive material, but you can save by buying in bulk. Figure $10 a quart but only $30 a gallon.

You can control its application by dabbing it on rather than brushing it on. Use a cloth.

The enemy of a remover is evaporation, so after applying the material to the wood or other surface, enclose the item in plastic to keep it relatively air tight. It will work longer.

There are various brands, but I like Bix for a simple reason: part of the product is salvageable. After use, scrape it and the finish off, then drop the glop in a screen in the shape of a cone and feed into a paint can. The remover will drain through the screen into the can, and the finish residue will remain. This way you can reuse about 30 percent of the product.

Paint Thinners

Back in the dark ages (when I was a professional housepainter), they used to sell paint thinners loose in 5-gallon cans. No more. Now it only comes packaged, in metal cans.

For exterior paint, I'd use steam-distilled (not gum) turpentine. Terp thins paint better and allows you to apply it more quickly, and it keeps the paint from setting up too quickly: you have more time to do touchups without the brush dragging.

For interior paint, look for bargains on odorless thinner, which, of course, is far from odorless. You can buy this stuff when it's on sale and safely store it; it has a very high flash point—it takes a lot to ignite it.

Plaster

This comes in a variety of sizes, but the 5-pound bag is best.

The big bugaboo of plaster is that it dries too quickly. To retard setting time, add a dash of vinegar to each batch you mix: this will triple the setting time (old-time painters used to add their urine to the paint which, one must admit, is even cheaper than using vinegar).

Plaster is for large holes and cracks. For medium-size holes I would suggest you use prepared spackling compound. But to save money, fill the hole $9/10$ ths with plaster which is a lot cheaper, then finish with the far more workable spackling compound.

Rust Removers

Rust remover—such as Naval Jelly—is expensive and many times does not have to be used. Just scrape or brush rust away (with a wire brush), or simply use a good red lead primer, such as the material Benjamin Moore makes.

If you want to remove rust without a primer, use muriatic *acid*. This is cheap and is mixed with water. It works well. Muriatic acid also takes rust stains off concrete. Safety should be observed, as detailed on containers.

Sandpaper

Sandpaper comes in various shades and forms, but the cheapest way to buy it is by the sheet. It's commonly available and you can expect to save 10 percent to 15 percent over buying it packaged.

Another way to save is to cut your own paper from sheets to fit the sander rather than buying the prepared pads. For example, I compared the cost of two sheets of paper, which were cut up into six sheets—exactly what was available by package—to see which cost more. The two sheets cost about $1, and the packaged cost $1.70. As the sheets get coarser in grade the savings become less because the coarser sheets cost more while the package price remains the same.

Stain

Sales are periodically run on exterior stains, and savings can be significant. The best months are usually October and November. The reason: stain is composed of a pig-

Cutting up sheets of sandpaper for use with a finish sander can be 25 percent cheaper than buying it pre-cut by the package.

---

ment and vehicle or solvent, and if the cans are sitting on the shelves over the winter the pigment will settle to the bottom of the can and may be difficult to mix properly come springtime. Hence, dealers want to get rid of it before this can occur.

You can buy these stains. Some oil-based stains may be used despite very low temperatures (in the 30s). You can store them over the winter by first turning them upside down so that any pigment that has settled will redistribute itself.

My top choice is Cabot.

Tapes

The big idea in saving money on tape is to use just what is required by the job and no more.

One useful diy tape is masking tape. This comes in various qualities at, of course, various prices. If you are using it, say, to bond pieces of paper or some similarly simple job, you could buy the low-end tape. If you are using the tape as a masker, say when applying different colors of paint to something, then you should get high-quality material.

Masking tape comes ¾", 1", 1½" and 2" wide. For quality tape expect to pay about $3 a roll; for lower-end material you'd only pay half that.

Whatever quality you use, if you plan to remove the tape do so within 24 hours. As time goes by this tape can virtually weld itself in place, and if you take it off after a long time, the paint or whatever else is beneath it will come off too.

Duct tape is a gray, cloth-like tape that was originally used to seal the seams in ductwork. But it is now used in a wide variety of jobs, wherever a strong tape is needed. Duct tapes comes in various widths and lengths. The shorter the roll, the more you pay.

As with masking tape, use the lower quality material for lesser jobs, and the higher quality material for jobs where it is required. Good quality duct tape costs around $3.69 for a 60-yard roll.

Wallcoverings

Once there was this simple thing called wallpaper. It was paper on which was printed a design in color. It was glued in place on the wall or ceiling.

Those days are gone forever. Today wallpaper—the standard material—is just one of a group of materials that are more accurately called wallcoverings. Wallcoverings usually come 36 square feet to the roll but in various widths: 20½, 27, 36 and 54 inches. Some imported rolls only contain 28 square feet to the roll, an important consideration when calculating cost. You may order these "Euro" rolls thinking they are 36 square feet to the roll when they're only 28.

You can order single, double, and triple rolls.

Some wallcoverings must have paste applied; others come prepasted and only need to be wet before being hung to activate the paste. Some coverings are "dry strippable," meaning that they can be stripped off the wall when desired rather than having to steam them loose (dry strippable is a good choice for renters).

Paper is the cheapest wallcovering available. Vinyl wallcovering is paper with a thin coating of vinyl. Sanitas is an example of this. Or it may be very heavy material which simulates grass, suede, or wood, and is coated with a protective layer of vinyl.

Wallcoverings is one area in which large discounts are possible. First, you can get discounts for wallcovering patterns that have not sold, or have gone out of vogue. You can ask a retailer if he has any of these. Discounts of 50 to 60 percent are not unreasonable.

Another way is to simply ask for a discount. If you are dealing with a store that specializes in selling paint and wallcoverings, you can ask for 30 percent. If you are dealing with a home center, you can ask them to give it to you at the sale price.

There are a number of other ways to save. One is to select a paper with little waste. There are three kinds of paper: drop match, random match, and straight match, as shown in the drawings. The drop match involves the most waste, so if possible pick another type of pattern. Failing this, consult closely with your dealer for the most efficient, waste-free way to hang it.

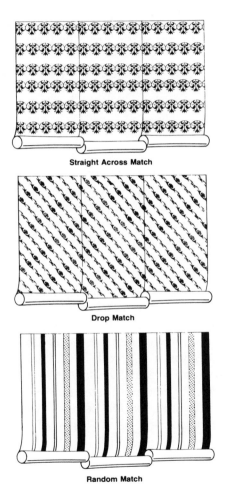

Straight Across Match

Drop Match

Random Match

Drop match paper involves the most waste when hanging, so you can save by getting one of the other types.

In terms of hanging a wallcovering, you should not use prepared pastes—they're far more expensive than products that you mix with water. Details are above under Adhesives.

Also, you don't need to buy a wallcovering brush to help you smooth paper. An ordinary large sponge works beautifully.

Costs: Grasscloth, top quality, $1.60 per square foot; medium vinyl, $.75 per square foot.

Weather Strip

A tremendous variety of weather strip is available for doors and windows, but the following are recommendations for the best bargains, generally speaking.

For doors, I would go for the strips of wood with foam edges. These come in a kit with two 7'-long pieces for the sides of the door and a 3' piece for across the top. They are tacked on with brads to seal the gap around the door (instructions come on the package). The cost is $5.60 to $6.50. Moorflex is one maker.

Another good product is Mortite, a pressure-sensitive foam which is stuck in place around the door. Cost is $2.89 to $4.89 for a 17' roll. This latter material can also be used on cellar windows. Mortite comes in different widths for various installation situations.

For standard windows, felt secured with small brads works well. It only costs $2.00 for a 25' roll.

Wood Putty

Wood putty comes in prepared form and as a powder, such as Durham's Rock Hard Wood Putty, that you mix with water. The Durham's is the far better buy, costing about one-fourth of what prepared stuff costs, and mixing it up is a piece of cake. It is an excellent wood putty.

Here, Plastic Wood costs almost $6. Durham's, at right, containing more material, costs only $1.59.

8

BURIED TREASURE

 A phenomenon of the last 20 years or so has been the emergence of the garage or tag sale, and it can be the source of a variety of excellent bargains for the do-it-yourselfer on any kind of product or material one can mention, and on both new and used products. Tools, hardware, building supply staples such as plywood and particleboard—you name it, it can be found at these sales. Really, buried treasures.

The tools, in particular, needn't be new for them to represent excellent value, because it is relatively easy, by replacing some parts, to rejuvenate them. More about that a little later.

First, though, a few tips on shopping garage sales. These are gleaned from one of the greatest garage sale

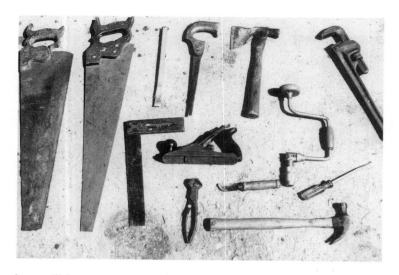

Incredibly, every one of these tools was purchased at a garage sale. They were bought by my friend "Crazy Walter" Hartten, who ain't so crazy.

shoppers ever to cast her legendary shadow across a driveway: Catherine, my wife.

"Sometimes," Catherine counsels, "picking up a bargain is a random thing. You go to the sale and find some tools or the like there. I would say that in maybe 40 percent of the cases you'd find things like that. Maybe 10 percent of these are tools and the rest are electrical, hardware, plumbing supplies. A hodgepodge.

"The other kind are sales that advertise tools. In these maybe 30 percent of the items are rolls and other do-it-yourself products."

And at which would you get the better buy generally?

"It doesn't matter," Catherine says, "the buys vary from garage sale to garage sale, whether they advertise or not.

"Generally, you can expect to pay around 20 percent of the retail price for any used diy product. If an item cost $5 retail you'd get it for a dollar. The new stuff might be a little more."

One wonders, of course, why someone would have brand-new tools or other stuff available at a garage sale. Did these, as they say, "fall off the back of a truck"?

"No," Catherine says, "a lot of people who have new stuff for sale are moving and don't want to take new items with them, which they will have no use for."

Before buying any tool that is driven by gas or electricity, test it. In rare instances a seller will try to rip off customers by selling them non-functioning items, but in some cases the sellers just assume they work, when they don't.

As mentioned, just because a tool is old or damaged doesn't mean it's worthless. Quite the contrary. Good tools can last virtually forever, given a little attention in the form of a new handle or new edges.

New handles can be bought for all kinds of hammers, for example—claw, framing, sledge and ball peen—and in various sizes. Figure $2 to $4 per handle, depending on what you buy.

Half hatchets and axes can also be affixed with new handles.

A variety of tools whose edges have seen better days can also not only be sharpened up, but can have a new edge put on, even new teeth. Says Walter "Crazy Walter" Hartten, ace sharpener of W & W Sharpall in Northport, Long Island, "Lots of tools can be brought back to life. I have resharpened saws that are over 100 years old. The

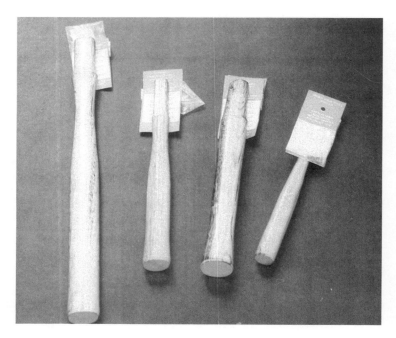

Many different tools can be resuscitated. New handles come in a variety of shapes and sizes.

only time a tool isn't worth sharpening is when the metal is so old it's brittle."

Walter furnished the following list of tools that can be resuscitated, and the prices he would charge.

■ Steel circular saw blades: Overall, they would cost $1.50 to $4 to sharpen. Specifically:
  6″ to 8″—$1.50
  9″ to 10″—$2.15
  12″ to 14″—$3
  16″ to 18″—$4

Walter says that such blades can be sharpened a half dozen times and more before having to be discarded. You might pay $20 to $30 if you bought the blades new. In essence, you can save over 1000 percent on some blades.

■ Carbide-tipped circular saw blades. There are two different kinds of carbide tips: synthetic or pure carbide, with the latter the far better quality.

Walter says he would charge anywhere from $3 to $11 depending on how many teeth the blade had. And he could successfully sharpen it around 10 times.

■ Hand saws. Nine of ten saws, Walter says, are perfectly okay for sharpening. He charges $1.75 to sharpen and $3.75 to retooth a blade.

■ Chisels. Wood chisels can also be given a new edge. Charge: 50 cents to $3.

■ Tin snips. These also can be sharpened at least twice. Cost: $2. New, the tool would set you back $9 to $20, depending on the kind you buy.

■ Drill bits: High-speed steel bits would cost 25 cents to $4. Spade and auger bits would cost $1 and up. A Forstner bit (which plumbers use to drill holes in framing) would cost $2.50 and up. It can usually be sharpened three times.

■ Axes. To sharpen: $3 and up.

■ Screwdrivers. These also can be reground and given a new edge for $1.

■ Chain saws. Here, Walter charges $3.50 to $7. To buy a chain in a store would set you back about $6.50 a foot, depending on style.

■ Cold chisels. These also can be given a new edge for $1.

■ Scrapers. These too can be given a new edge: 50¢.

You may have some treasures in your own home,

long-broken or unused tools that are rusty and dull-edged . . .

Walter is waiting.

9

SOME FINAL THOUGHTS

 I hope the previous chapters have provided readers with the detailed shopping info needed to get products and material at good discounts. But there are a few other things I have to say that, I think, may also be helpful in shopping.

One is to simply realize, as bizarre as it sounds, that *money* is to be saved. Somehow, for some people, just seeing numbers doesn't impart this. Saving money remains an abstract concept.

I would suggest these folks think of money saved in terms of what it can buy. If, for example, you save $300 buying a Kohler toilet, that's $300 toward your dental bill, or for a kid's clothing, or for that vacation you always wanted to take, or to put in the bank. Take the money out of the abstract and into your hand, where you can see it.

Another thing: stay involved. It is very important to become fully involved in seeking out good buys, but it is also important to *stay with it.* Calling people cold and asking for prices is difficult for some people, and one's tendency can be to walk away from it before the absolute best price has been gleaned.

Here, if the process gets to be bothersome, a pain in you know what, then put it on the shelf for a while and come back with renewed energy when you feel up to it.

One other thing is this, and it reiterates what we said earlier in the book: there are bargains out there, wonderful bargains—if you are willing to go after them. That's all you really have to do.

Good shopping!

APPENDIX A

WARRANTIES AND GUARANTEES

As a shopper, you should check to see if a manufacturer provides a guarantee or warranty (which means the same thing) on his product or material. While it can't give you an absolute indication, it does indicate to some degree how much he believes in his product or material. No company—except a fly-by-night one—is going to guarantee something that it feels is going to come back to haunt it.

There are two kinds of warranties, limited and full, but even though a warranty says that it is full that doesn't mean that it guarantees everything. It's a good idea, if it is an expensive item, to read the warranty *before* buying the product. You might learn some interesting details. For example, if you were buying a whirlpool bath, the warranty might guarantee everything until the whirlpool is filled with water—then the company's responsibility ceases.

I'm joshing, of course, but the warranty can give you insight into the product, and if warranties differ from one company to the other, that can tell you something too, can't it?

One vital point: manufacturers' warranties universally demand that their products be installed their way—or else the warranty is null and void. For example, as mentioned earlier in the book, some wooden doors must be painted on all four edges by the buyer for the warranty against swelling to be valid. Many a diyer has learned this point too late. Therefore, before you install any product, read how the manufacturer wants it to be done.

Following is the full warranty of the Bird company for their fiberglass shingles, which happen to be a good product. Slog through it. It should help give you a sense of what a warranty is all about and how it can help you.

Bird
Incorporated

Limited Warranty Against Leakage
Plus Five Year Limited Wind Warranty

I. COVERAGE

Bird Incorporated (Bird) warrants to you that subject to the terms and conditions set forth below, the Bird Shingles you have purchased are free from manufacturing defects that cause leaks in your roof under normal exposure conditions during the prescribed Warranty Period, as specified for each product below.

II. LIMITED WARRANTY AGAINST LEAKAGE

If leaks caused by manufacturing defects in the Bird shingles are discovered, Bird will contribute a pro-rated portion of the repair or replacement cost; based on a maximum contribution of $2.00 per square. A square is equal to the number of shingles necessary to cover 100 square feet.

A pro-rated contribution will be determined by multiplying a maximum amount of $2.00 per square times the number of years, including partial years, remaining in the Warranty Period at the time of repair or replacement; however, such contribution will not exceed in total, a maximum amount equal to the original installed cost of the materials covered.

Bird will not pay for:

A. Any costs for the tear off or removal of any shingles or related roofing materials including, but not limited to, metal work or flashing.

B. Or, any expenditure that may be incurred in replacing or repairing shingle prior to written acknowledgement of Bird's responsibility.

III. WARRANTY PERIOD

This Limited Warranty against leakage is valid during the applicable Warranty Period as specified below. The Warranty Period commences on the date of installation of the shingles.

CHART

Product	Total Warranty Period	Monthly Reduction
Architect 90	30 years (360 Months)	1/360
Woodscape	25 years (300 Months)	1/300
Mark 80	30 years (360 Months)	1/360
Fireline	30 years (360 Months)	1/360
Seal King	25 years (300 Months)	1/300
Jet 80	20 years (240 Months)	1/240
Wind Seal 80	20 years (240 Months)	1/240

During the Limited Warranty Period, Bird will not pay for the tear off or removal of any shingles or related roofing material including, but not limited to, metal work or flashing, when such removal is contrary to accepted roofing practices as published by the Asphalt Roofing Manufactures Association. Any cost in excess of Bird's calculated contribution will be the owner's responsibility.

IV. LIMITED FIVE YEAR WIND RESISTANCE WARRANTY

Bird warrants that its shingles will not blow off in winds of less than 54 miles per hour if they have been properly installed. Your shingles contain a strip of thermal sealing asphalt which must be exposed to warm sunlight for several days in order to seal completely. Shingles which are installed in the fall or winter may not be exposed to sufficient sunlight and may not adequately seal down until spring. Shingles which are not exposed to direct sunlight or to adequate surface temperatures may never seal. Shingles which do not seal because they have been exposed to inadequate sealing conditions will not be considered to have been properly installed.

If the Bird shingles covered by this warranty blow off within five years after the date of installation, Bird will supply replacement shingles without charge, and will pay the reasonable cost of manually sealing any unsealed Bird shingles remaining on your roof. Bird will not pay for the cost of removal, application and installation of replacement shingles.

This five year limited wind warranty does not cover the removal, application or installation of the replacement shingles, nor damage attributable to other causes, including, but not limited to those causes set forth under Limitations and Exclusions.

V. LIMITATIONS AND EXCLUSIONS ON YOUR WARRANTY COVERAGE

BIRD EXCLUDES AND WILL NOT PAY INCIDENTAL OR CONSEQUENTIAL DAMAGES (INCLUDING, WITHOUT LIMITATION, INJURY TO PERSONS OR THE COST OF REPAIRING OR REPLACING OTHER PROPERTY WHICH IS DAMAGED WHEN THE ROOF LEAKS).

PLEASE NOTE: SOME STATES DO NOT ALLOW FOR THE EXCLUSION OF LIMITATION OF INCIDENTAL AND CONSEQUENTIAL DAMAGES, SO THE ABOVE LIMITATION MAY NOT APPLY TO YOU.

This warranty gives you specific legal rights and you may also have other rights which vary from state to state. Except for these other rights, the remedies provided under this warranty state the limits of Bird's responsibilities.

This Warranty does not cover other products (such as flashing or metal work) and Bird will not be responsible for damage to the shingles which is attributable in whole or in part to other causes, including but not limited to:

1. Faulty installation not in accordance with Bird's written instructions;
2. Hurricane, tornado, gale, lightning, flood, or other violent or unusual phenomena of the elements;
3. Wind velocities greater than 54 mph (Beaufort Scale **No. 9**);
4. Fire and other casualties;
5. Settlement, distortion, failure, or cracking of the roof, deck, walls, or foundation of the building;
6. Defect in or failure of flashing, metal work or material used as a roof base over which Bird shingles or other materials are applied;
7. Damage to the Bird shingles due to any cause other than manufacturing defects;
8. Misuse of or negligent or improper storage of Bird shingles
9. Equipment installation, structural changes, or any other alternations in the roof after application of the Bird shingles or other materials;
10. Defects originating in portions of the building unrelated to workmanship and materials supplied as part of the roofing contract;
11. Improper ventilation;
12. Variations in color (shading) which may occur from the positioning of granular surfacing materials in the materials (Directional Shading);
13. Traffic on or over the roof or impact of foreign objects;

VI. REPLACEMENT SHINGLES

Any replacement shingles provided by Bird in settlement of claims will be warranted for the balance of the original warranty period as though purchased and installed at the time of installation of the shingles which have been replaced. Bird reserves the right to discontinue and/or make changes in any of its products. If products identical to those covered by this warranty are not available, Bird reserves the right to substitute products of like quality.

VII. HOW TO MAKE A WARRANTY CLAIM

To make a claim under this Warranty, simply notify Bird Incorporated (preferably in writing) at Bird Roofing Products, Inc., 1077 Pleasant St., Norwood, MA 02062 within a reasonable period of time after discovery of the defect (Bird considers 30 days to be a reasonable time), together with proof of purchase of the Bird shingles and the installation date. You must give Bird reasonable opportunity to inspect the shingles and be provided with samples before any remedial steps are taken. Following such investigation, Bird will promptly perform its obligation under this Warranty.

Please take a moment to complete and mail the attached Registration and Acknowledgement Card. It will help establish the date of purchase and installation. Failure to mail the card will not affect your warranty coverage.

VIII. EFFECTIVE DATE AND TRANSFERABILITY

This Shingle Warranty is only in effect for shingles purchased after August 1, 1991.

This Warranty is transferable to a new owner and subject to the terms and conditions explained.

Please use this space to record vital information regarding your roofing installation. Please print in ink or type.

Owner's Name

Street & No.

City,   State,   Zip

Contractor or Supplier Name

City,   State,   Zip

Cost of Roofing Materials & Labor	Completion Date	No. Sqs.	Color

Type of Shingle

☐ Architect 90	30 years	☐ Jet 80	20 years	☐ Fireline	30 year
☐ Woodscape	25 years	☐ Wind Seal 80	20 years	☐ Seal King	25 years
☐ Mark 80	30 years				

APPENDIX B

METALS AND FINISHES

Metal is, of course, the main material used for hardware of all kinds, and it's a good idea to understand what the various qualities and characteristics of the metals are, as well as the finishes. It's information that can help you make a better buying decision. For example, you may see an item, say a hinge, that you like in brass, but you won't buy it because brass is too expensive. Meanwhile, you can get a very similar look—at much lower cost—by buying the same item brass-plated.

The following is a roundup.

Black Iron, This is iron just the way it looks when manufactured, before any finishing is done.

Brass. This is a soft, yellowish brown metal with excellent resistance to weather, though it eventually can oxidize and turn green. Brass costs double the price of steel. A pair of $5 steel hinges would easily cost you more than $10 in pure brass.

Brass-plated. This is steel with a brass coating. It resists weather, but it's not weatherproof, and costs about the same as plain steel.

Bright. Once this referred to items, such as nails, that were naturally polished during manufacturing, and were dubbed "bright" finished. Today, nails are still bright but this usually is because they are given a zinc wash during manufacture.

Bronze. This is a hard brownish metal that is even more resistant to weather and water than brass and costs three times as much as steel.

Bronze-plated is steel coated with bronze. Such items will stand up well to weather, but the main idea behind the coating seems to be looks. Items coated with bronze have a soft luster that is attractive and, as with brass coated, the cost is greatly reduced.

Cadmium-plated. This is the same as coating items with zinc. The terms are interchangeable. The finish produced is bright and somewhat weather-resistant.

Chrome-plated. Most people think that chrome plating is for bath fittings only, but a number of other items, including hinges, come this way. As such, a chrome-plated item stands up to moisture very well.

Copper. This soft brownish metal is never surpassed as water pipe.

Copper-plated. Just what it says. Steel that has been given a coating of copper.

Drop-forged steel. Many tools are drop forged. It is a process wherein molten steel is "dropped" into a mold and allowed to dry. Drop forging is a favorite way to make cheaper tools. While it's fine for most tools, think twice about getting a hammer that has been drop forged; it may break under strenuous use (such as pounding nails into masonry).

Electro-galvanized. This is really a ripoff term, because it makes it seem as if items have been galvanized—which makes them totally weatherproof—when in fact they have not been. Imports from China and Taiwan are more than occasionally referred to as electro-galvanized.

Galvanized. Here, items—mainly nails, screws, and bolts—are given a bath in hot zinc (they are "hot dipped"), and this makes them impervious to weather. Characteristically, a truly galvanized item has a dull, gray, rough finish. Electro-plated or non-galvanized items have a shiny finish.

Buying galvanized items is expensive—a third to twice as much as buying non-galvanized—so you should make sure you need the weatherproof feature. If you don't, save your money.

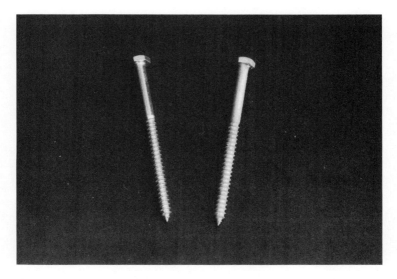

If you need a weatherproof item, make sure it's weatherproof. The bolt at left is shiny and is not. The one on the right, dull, gray, and rough, is galvanized.

Nickel-plated. Here, items have been coated with a combination of chrome and zinc to make them better looking and more durable than they might otherwise be.

Oiled. This is not a finish per se, but a coating given to hardware to keep it from rusting while waiting to be sold.

Stainless steel. Just what it says. Comes in various glosses, but beware of items that are labeled "non-rusting metal" or the like. Indeed, this cheap material won't rust but it will stain.

Zinc-coated. As mentioned above, the same as cadmium-plated.